WHAT TO EAT
NEXT

'This is the kind of food I particularly like – uncomplicated, a simple delivery of true joy to the heart of the table.'

WHAT TO EAT
NEXT

Valentine Warner

Mitchell Beazley

For my beautiful son Louis. I only hope to nourish both your stomach and soul along the winding way – a sunny path with a warm breeze at your back. I love you always.

What to Eat Next

by Valentine Warner

First published in Great Britain in 2014 by Mitchell Beazley,
an imprint of Octopus Publishing Group Limited,
Endeavour House, 189 Shaftesbury Avenue, London WC2H 8JY.
www.octopusbooks.co.uk

An Hachette UK Company
www.hachette.co.uk

Note: This book contains some dishes made with raw or lightly cooked eggs.
It is prudent for more vulnerable people, such as pregnant and nursing mothers,
people with weakened immune systems, the elderly, babies and young children
to avoid dishes made with uncooked or lightly cooked eggs.

The author has asserted his moral rights.

ISBN: 978 1 84533 542 7

A CIP record for this book is available from the British Library.

Set in Chronicle Deck, Chronicle Display and Helvetica Neue.

Printed and bound in China.

Art Director: Jonathan Christie
Head of Editorial: Tracey Smith
Art Direction, Design (including jacket) and Props Styling: Pene Parker
Senior Editor: Leanne Bryan
Photographer: Chris Terry
Food Stylists: Sunil Vijayaker, Katie Giovanni and Georgie Besterman
Recipe Testers: Justine Pattison and Lauren Brignell
Copy Editor: Annie Lee
Proofreaders: Ruth Baldwin and Kate Quarry
Indexer: Isobel McLean
Senior Production Manager: Katherine Hockley

Introduction

What to Eat Next is a question constantly emblazoned across my mind. Well, not constantly, but certainly with more frequency than regular mealtimes. My wife is perturbed by this, and by my propensity for discussing future meals while eating the one that's being served up. But cooking is my job, a love; after all, I'm not a musician, mathematician or architect, and anyway, what to eat next has surely been the first question on humankind's mind since its first naked, rain-lashed day on this rumbling, lava-streaked Earth. Thousands of years of muddy fingernails and grubbing for roots – or rooting for grubs, for that matter – will always lie deep in our bones. As a child I bit everything in order to understand how the world was put together. I'm distracted by a glimpse of mushrooms on the verge as I drive by, always have a fishing rod in the car and can never resist a market. How else was it going to turn out?

So I reply that a day needs planning, and I like to look forward to lunchtime sardines on toast (*see* page 112) and smile when a peep into the fridge reveals rib of beef and fried artichokes (*see* page 34) for dinner. A sunrise spin to the local shop for bacon and eggs might be in order, I think, as I fall asleep.

In my case, repetition only feeds a dull mind, as I like variety on my table, sometimes driven by the most precise cravings – grilled liver (*see* page 51) or baked shallots in cream (*see* page 139). Were I to be reborn as an animal I would choose the grizzly bear. A bit of meat, plenty of fish, ants clawed from their frantic hill, mushrooms, some berries and honey to satisfy any sugary cravings.

This was originally meant to be one of those save-you-time books. 'I suppose you want me to call it *Speedy Greedy*,' I quipped sarcastically. 'Brilliant,' replied my publisher. But I simply couldn't write that book – I don't eat like that.

Nevertheless, we came to a compromise. How long did I think it was acceptable to wait for food? 'One hour or less,' I replied. There are a few exceptions – three or four long-players – but otherwise this book is full of things you can whip up in a flash or cook in the sort of time I used to spend eagerly watching my parents prepare food from beginning to end, knowing that they had hungry children to feed. If it's meals in minutes you want, you'll find some here, but there are also things you may want to cook more.

So here is my fourth collection of time-honoured classics, comforters for nights when the rat-tat-tat rain persists, recipes from my travels, the fun, the under-one-hour. It proclaims my undying passion for fish and for a good breakfast far away from cereal-box city.

It has taken me a day to write this introduction – it's 11.13pm and I'm ravenous. So what to eat next? Well, the half a cooked chicken leg that's meant for my daughter's lunch (naughty daddy), two slices of Cheddar with some curried pickle and a Percy Pig sweet should do me just fine.

Meat

Cream of chicken and leek soup

This smooth, creamy, velvety soup offers the same comfort for cold weather as a box of hankies for the weeping.

The recipe is all about homemade stock. I would always advocate making your own stock, as bought brands tend to be insipid, and this recipe starts from the standpoint that the stock has been made already. A note here for when making a chicken stock from the wreckage of Sunday lunch: before you begin it's imperative that you explore the inside of the chicken and take out any lemon, which will make the stock bitter, then give the inside a rinse.

I often see people boiling the bones for an eternity, but you can't extract any more flavour from a chicken frame than it will give you in 2 hours. Second, let the water wobble away rather than watch the carcass bump around in furious bubbles. Gentleness will prevent the stock becoming greasy as well as misty. Next, SKIM OFTEN!

If you have any cooked chicken meat left over from a Sunday roast, then all the better, but it's not essential.

Serves 4–6 (makes 1 litre)

› 2 medium leeks, any chewy outer layers and root removed
› 50g unsalted butter
› a small scratch of nutmeg
› a smidgen of dried thyme
› 4 tablespoons plain white flour, sifted
› 750ml good strong chicken stock with proper taste
› 300ml full-fat milk
› 1 heaped teaspoon flaked sea salt
› 2 good handfuls of cooked chicken meat that has been picked from a Sunday roast, pulled into strips or diced (optional)
› 100ml cream
› the faintest squeeze of fresh lemon juice, to give an edge but no more
› ground white pepper
› hot buttered toast, to serve (optional)

1. Slice the leeks into 5mm rounds and wash thoroughly to remove grit and oomska.

2. Gently sauté the leeks in a large pot with the butter, nutmeg, thyme, and a good dusting of ground white pepper until softened, while keeping a nice green colour to the leek tops – about 8 minutes. Do not brown.

3. Stir the flour into the leeks and cook out its taste for a further minute or so. Do not burn the flour.

4. Now start slowly adding the stock. The mixture will get very thick before it starts to loosen again.

5. Follow with the milk and allow the mixture to simmer gently for a further 10 minutes. The leeks should be totally soft.

6. Season with the sea salt and add more white pepper to taste.

7. Add the chicken meat, if using, and cream and, when you see the faintest simmering around the edges of the broth, squeeze in a few drops of lemon and taste – it should only just be noticeable.

8. Serve immediately with hot buttered toast, if liked.

Notes on chicken noodle soup

This soup is often overcomplicated, with too many bits and bobs included and more resembling a minestrone. All it needs is a good stock and vermicelli. I would not advise making it with ready-made vacuum packs of stock, as I have yet to find one that's as good as one home made.

See *page 10 for advice on making stock from the carcass of a chicken roasted with a lemon inside it.*

Tremble the chicken carcass, with whatever you may have, in roughly 3 litres of water. Maybe 1 medium onion – skin left on, and cut in quarters – a celery stick or parsley stalks, a smidgen of thyme, 2 chopped medium carrots and a few cloves of garlic. Mind you, just chicken, salt and water will make an excellent broth. Leave the lid on and, to reiterate, let the stock wobble rather than boil for a couple of hours.

Skim the broth of scum and fat carefully when need be. Remember that any jelly from the chicken should be peeled off the plate and plopped into the stock as well. Stocks tend to be underseasoned and need a little more salt than you'd imagine to bring out the taste.

I suggest using 80g of vermicelli (around 4 nests) to 1 litre of stock, and breaking the noodles before cooking or snipping them with scissors afterwards.

I like to cook the noodles separately in water and then transfer them to the broth rather than muddy the waters. My only addition to the soup would be a little finely chopped parsley and maybe a little squeeze of lemon juice. Add a healthy bombing of black pepper before eating.

'I have yet to find a ready-made stock that's as good as one home made.'

Bang-bang chicken salad

Quite often there is too much salad in a recipe like this one, which over-dilutes the fun sauce and makes for a boring plate. Never a fan of the Chinese beansprout, I've left them out where others put them in.

Makes a light lunch for 2 or a bigger lunch for 1

> 1/3 large cucumber, peeled, seeds scooped out and medium diced
> 1 teaspoon flaked sea salt
> 1 large skinless chicken breast
> 2 large cloves of garlic, skin left on, split lengthways
> 8 black peppercorns
> 2 teaspoons Japanese soy sauce
> 2 medium carrots, peeled, then shaved into ribbons with a potato peeler
> 2 spring onions, thinly sliced on a steep diagonal
> 1 finger-length hot green chilli, finely sliced
> 12 small fresh mint leaves
> a good handful of fresh coriander leaves
> 1 tablespoon sesame seeds, toasted

For the sauce

> 4 tablespoons smooth peanut butter
> the juice from 1 large thumb-sized piece of fresh ginger that has been peeled and finely grated
> 2 teaspoons Japanese soy sauce
> 2 1/2 tablespoons toasted sesame oil
> 1 tablespoon dark runny honey or soft brown sugar (not muscovado)
> 1 1/2 tablespoons Chinese black vinegar or other rice wine vinegar (preferably not white), plus extra for dressing the veg and chicken

1. Put the cucumber into a colander with the sea salt and leave to drip until the last minute.

2. Put the chicken breast, garlic cloves and peppercorns in as small a pan as the chicken will comfortably fit. Snug is good. Only just cover the chicken breast with cold water, then add the soy sauce. Bring to a simmer, then turn down to barely a wobble and cook the chicken for 8 minutes, skimming when need be.

3. While the chicken cooks, put everything for the sauce into a bowl and mix well.

4. Remove the chicken to a plate to cool. Fish out the garlic from the broth, then turn up the heat and rapidly reduce the broth until only 3 tablespoons are left. Allow to cool.

5. Loosen the sauce with 1 tablespoon of the cooled broth.

6. Slice the chicken lengthways, chop it into large matchsticks and place in a mixing bowl with the carrots, spring onions, chilli, drained cucumber, and the mint and coriander leaves (keeping a few back for the garnish).

7. Dress the veg and chicken with the remainder of the cold broth and a splash more of the vinegar.

8. Pile the salad lightly on the plates, shaking off any excess dressing. Scatter over the sesame seeds, then divide the sauce over the top.

Harissa

This flavoursome Tunisian chilli purée is an accompaniment for many North African dishes. Fabulous with tagines, merguez sausages and bean or lentil soups, it should be approached with some respect. One popular brand, Le Phare Du Cap Bon, comes in a squeezy metal tube that can be planted in place of toothpaste, to fool sleepy morning risers. Hilarious... NOT.

Many Western recipes omit the caraway, which is disappointing as I find it the very ingredient that makes this sauce so particularly interesting and delicious. I have added a splash of rose water too, for that extra floral note. Smeared all over the inside of some broken-off baguette and with a fried chorizo shoved in, it makes a brilliantly simple and bang-on sandwich. Excellent served alongside the Poussin with Green Olives and Preserved Lemons on page 22, or with Ibrahim's Merguez on page 42.

Serves 6 as a condiment

› 12 finger-length hot red chillies
› 1½ teaspoons coriander seeds
› ½ teaspoon cumin seeds
› ½ teaspoon caraway seeds
› 3 cloves of garlic
› ½ teaspoon flaked sea salt
› 2 teaspoons tomato purée (optional)
› ½ teaspoon fresh lemon juice
› 1 tablespoon olive oil (not extra virgin, as it will flavour the harissa too heavily)
› 7 drops of rose water (optional)

1. Preheat the grill to high.

2. Place the chillies in a roasting tray and put them under the grill until their skins brown and blister. Turn them over and grill the other side. Allow them to cool before peeling and deseeding them.

3. In a small frying pan, gently toast the coriander, cumin and caraway seeds, swirling them often, for about 2 minutes, until fragrant to the nose. Keep them moving, as it is essential they do not burn. Grind the seeds to a fine powder in a pestle and mortar or in a spice grinder.

4. Chop the garlic finely and scatter the sea salt over it. Mash the two together with the side of a knife blade until well puréed.

5. In a bowl with a stick blender or using the pestle and mortar, blend the chillies with the spices, tomato purée (if using) and garlic until very smooth. Stir in the lemon juice, followed by the olive oil. Add the rose water, if using, and correct the seasoning if need be.

6. Allow the flavours to combine for 1 hour before using.

Piri piri chicken wings

Here is my confession. Frequently I can be found at a dark corner table in Nando's stripping the meat off their peri peri chicken wings, with burning lips and a greasy face. Sometimes I do the work in a quiet backstreet – eating my way home. My guilt lies in that I should probably be making them myself, given my job, but purism can be terribly tedious. Here is my own recipe for them, very good too but not as instant.

The stumpy red piri piri chillies are not always easy to find, so replace them with the Dutch red variety you will usually find in the supermarket.

Serves 4

› 1¹/2 tablespoons groundnut or sunflower oil
› 10 finger-length hot red chillies, stalks removed
› 75ml red wine vinegar
› juice of 1 lime
› 2 teaspoons fresh thyme leaves
› 5 cloves of garlic
› 3 teaspoons flaked sea salt
› 24 plump chicken wings

1. Put everything apart from the chicken into a blender and blitz the hell out of it.

2. Score the chicken wings lightly all over with a sharp knife. Pour the marinade over the chicken wings in a non-metallic bowl and leave them to marinate in the fridge for 2 hours.

3. Light the barbecue charcoals about 20 minutes before cooking, and, when they are pulsing white and orange, place the wings on the grill. Cook them for approximately 10–15 minutes, turning every so often and each time brushing them with more of the remaining marinade, until well browned and slightly charred (not burnt).

4. Eat with French fries, coleslaw, cold beer and music.

'Eat with French fries, coleslaw, cold beer and music.'

Jubilee chicken

Writing this book during the Queen's 60th year on the throne, I felt I had to include this recipe, a revamped coronation chicken, to celebrate. The recipe was developed for a street party thrown by Nyetimber sparkling wine and served to 200 happy subjects sitting along the length of an apparently endless crooked table draped in white linen.

Serves 4–6

> 2 teaspoons garam masala
> 1½ teaspoons flaked sea salt
> 1 excellent chicken (I recommend a Suffolk White from Sutton Hoo), jointed into 8 pieces (your butcher will do this for you if necessary)
> 25g unsalted butter
> 1 tablespoon sunflower oil
> 3 tablespoons flaked almonds
> a small bunch of fresh curly parsley, leaves chopped
> a small bunch of fresh mint, leaves chopped

For the Jubilee sauce

> 70g unsalted butter
> 1 large onion, very finely chopped
> 1 thumb-sized piece of fresh ginger, peeled and very finely grated
> 1 bay leaf
> a pinch of grated nutmeg
> 4 cardamom pods, seeds removed and crushed, husks discarded
> a small pinch of ground cloves
> a small pinch of good saffron
> ½ stick of cinnamon
> ½ teaspoon celery salt
> 1 teaspoon garam masala
> 2 heaped teaspoons mild curry powder (I recommend Bolst's)
> 2 tablespoons sweet vermouth
> 1 teaspoon Dijon or wholegrain mustard
> 1½ tablespoons mango chutney
> 2½ heaped tablespoons good-quality mayonnaise
> 2½ heaped tablespoons crème fraîche
> a squeeze of lemon juice (optional)
> ½ small sweet mango, such as Alphonso, diced (optional)

1. Mix the garam masala and sea salt together and rub into the skin of each of the chicken pieces.

2. Next make the sauce. Melt the butter in a pan and sauté the onion with the ginger, bay leaf, nutmeg, cardamom, cloves, saffron and cinnamon. Cook gently over a medium heat, stirring often, until the onion is meltingly tender and totally soft, about 10 minutes or so.

3. Now add the celery salt, garam masala and curry powder and cook the onion for a further couple of minutes, stirring often.

4. Pour in the vermouth and briskly simmer away until evaporated. Stir in the mustard and cook for 1 last minute. Leave the mixture to cool.

5. Stir in the mango chutney, mayonnaise and crème fraîche, remove the bay leaf and cinnamon stick, then use a blender to purée the sauce mixture until as smooth as possible. Check the seasoning one last time – you may want to add a squeeze of lemon juice if you feel it needs an edge.

6. Transfer the sauce back to the cold pan and stir in the fresh mango (if using); otherwise transfer the sauce to a gravy boat and cover until ready to serve.

7. Preheat the oven to 200°C/fan 180°C/gas 6.

8. Heat the butter and oil in a large, nonstick, ovenproof frying pan. Lay the chicken pieces in the pan, skin-side down. Fry over a medium-high heat for around 10 minutes, or until the skin is crisp and golden. Regulate the heat so as not to burn the butter or the chicken.

9. Transfer the pan to the oven and cook for a further 10 minutes, until the chicken is done. (If you don't have an ovenproof frying pan, just transfer the chicken to a baking tray instead.)

10. Put the chicken on a board or platter and leave to rest for 5 minutes or so.

11. While the chicken is resting, toast the almonds in a dry frying pan until golden. Scatter them over the chicken along with the parsley and mint.

12. Serve the chicken pieces with the Jubilee sauce.

Jubilee chicken

'Writing this book during the
Queen's 60th year on the throne,
I felt I had to include this recipe,
a revamped coronation chicken,
to celebrate.'

Poussin with mushrooms and Madeira

I rarely buy poussin because... come to think of it, I don't have an answer. There you go, Mother; see – I don't have an answer for everything! Once in a blue moon, though, I do remember that I'm in the mood for a baby chicken, always, as I now recall, when I'm on my own. The poussin will see me lay a formal little table for one, just so, with a bottle of wine opened and ready next to my place setting.

This recipe came to me simply on seeing a 1950s print on a French bistro toilet wall. All the ingredients, bar the Madeira, were in the picture. The poussins are excellent served on a slice of fried bread.

Serves 2

› 2 poussins, untrussed
› 3/4 teaspoon flaked sea salt
› 50g unsalted butter
› a splash of sunflower oil
› 12 chestnut mushrooms, quartered
› 2 small bay leaves
› 5 cloves of garlic, very finely sliced
› 125ml Madeira
› 100ml double cream
› 2 heaped tablespoons chopped fresh parsley

1. Season the poussins all over with the sea salt.

2. Heat the butter and oil in a frying pan and sear the poussins until golden brown all over. They should sizzle immediately on entering the pan. Regulate the heat so as not to burn the butter.

3. Take the pan off the heat and put the poussins side by side in a small casserole that owns a lid.

4. Preheat the oven to 190°C/ fan 170°C/gas 5.

5. Return the frying pan to the heat and add the mushrooms, along with the bay leaves. Sauté until any wateriness has gone and the mushrooms just begin to colour. Stir in the garlic and cook until just before it starts to catch. Tip the pan slightly and spoon off the excess fat.

6. Pour over the Madeira, bring to a simmer and cook the mushroom mixture for 1 minute more, stirring.

7. Spoon the mushrooms and Madeira around the poussins. Put the lid on the casserole.

8. Put the young chicks in the oven and cook for 40 minutes, or until done (pierce the thickest part of the thigh with a skewer – the juices should run clear).

9. Remove from the oven, then swirl in the cream and scatter over the parsley before serving.

Poussin with green olives and preserved lemons

Where I used to live, on the Golbourne Road in west London, is a little Moroccan restaurant. Frequenting this place I became a creature of habit – a very liberating feeling, I might add – as I only ever ordered two of the tagines: the lamb, prune, egg and almond (barkok) and this one. The proprietor used to guess which one I would be having. If he guessed wrongly he would smile and say, 'Next time.' He always guessed wrongly, or else some other strange psychological game was being acted out on me. I loved the cosy feeling that being a regular gives – it allows one to skip the whole menu-reading fluffery.

Make sure you have some fiery harissa to accompany this (*see* page 14), and serve with some cinnamon-dusted couscous. By the way, the tagine is the pot, not the stew. Any heavy casserole with a lid will do.

Serves 2–4

- a pinch of saffron
- 300ml warm water
- 2 poussins
- 1 heaped teaspoon ground turmeric
- 2 teaspoons ground ginger
- 3 tablespoons extra virgin olive oil
- 1 medium red onion, very finely chopped
- 4 cloves of garlic, finely grated
- 25g bunch of fresh coriander, including stalks, very finely chopped
- 1 large preserved lemon (around 75g), halved, deseeded and thinly sliced, plus 1–2 tablespoons of the liquid from the jar
- 125g good green pitted olives
- 1–1½ teaspoons flaked sea salt
- ground black pepper

To serve
- cinnamon-dusted couscous
- harissa (*see* page 14)

1. Put the saffron into a measuring jug and cover with the warm water. Leave to stand.

2. Split the poussins lengthways in half, as close to the breastbone as possible. Place skin-side up in a wide, shallow, flameproof casserole and sprinkle with the turmeric and ginger. Drizzle with the oil.

3. Mix together the red onion, garlic, coriander and preserved lemon and scatter over the poussins. Drop the olives on top. Season generously with the sea salt and a good grind of black pepper. Pour over the saffron-infused water and add the 1–2 tablespoons preserving liquid from the lemon jar.

4. Bring to a simmer on the hob. Cover with a lid and cook at a low simmer for 40 minutes, turning the poussins after 20 minutes. Check after 5 minutes, as the lid will increase the temperature, so correct the heat back to gentle simmering.

5. Serve the poussins with the couscous and harissa.

Grilled quails with almond mayonnaise

Little quails go so well with garlic mayonnaise. I would say, in this case, that the quails are best cooked over charcoal if you can, but I'm going to cook them under the grill here as this is probably more user-friendly.

Serves 2-3

> 6 quails
> olive oil, for rubbing
> 1 tablespoon dried thyme
> 2 teaspoons smoked hot paprika
> 2 teaspoons flaked sea salt

For the almond mayonnaise
> 1 good teaspoon Dijon mustard
> 2 teaspoons fresh lemon juice, plus extra, if necessary
> 3 fat cloves of garlic, finely chopped and smashed to a purée with a little flaked sea salt
> 2 free-range egg yolks
> 150ml sunflower oil
> 50ml extra virgin olive oil
> 40g flaked almonds
> flaked sea salt
> ground black pepper

1. Start by making the mayonnaise. Using a stick blender or a whisk in a bowl, whiz together the mustard, lemon juice, garlic and egg yolks.

2. Continue to blend or whisk as you pour in the sunflower oil slowly. Soon an emulsion will start to form and before long it will thicken. If the mayo is becoming thick but there is still oil left to add, let it down with a little warm water, but remember it should not be drippy, only just stiff.

3. Add the olive oil gradually. Taste the mayonnaise – it should be pretty punchy with garlic. Add a little more lemon juice, if necessary, and season to taste.

4. Toast the almonds, swirling them around a dry pan constantly over a medium heat until golden. Tip on to a plate to cool. Roughly chop them and add them to the mayonnaise.

5. Preheat the grill to high. Rub the quails all over with olive oil. Mix together the thyme, paprika and sea salt. Rub the mixture into each bird.

6. Lay the quails, breast-side up, on a rack sitting over a baking tray lined with aluminium foil. Put them under the grill, close enough that they brown but do not burn. Cook, turning as they brown, for about 12–14 minutes until done.

7. Remove the quails from the grill and allow them to rest for 5 minutes.

8. Serve with the almond mayo and a glass of cold sherry.

Duck legs with cucumber

When we think of duck legs we think of them either attached to a whole roasted bird or as a single confit leg – very delicious, but with a rather lengthy and greasy process of preparation. Here are straightforward roasted duck legs with a delicious cucumber accompaniment, perfect for a summer's day, as I think duck often gets put unfairly in the cold-weather eating category. Good eaten with new potatoes tossed with butter, some salt and pepper and maybe a little chopped dill.

Don't use table salt in place of the flaked sea salt when preparing the cucumber, as the amount would make it taste far too strong.

Serves 2

> 2 medium duck legs
> a little sunflower oil
> 1 teaspoon dried thyme
> 3 teaspoons flaked sea salt
> 1 medium cucumber, peeled, halved lengthways, deseeded and cut into 5mm slices
> 1/2 teaspoon coriander seeds, or 1 whole teaspoon if not using caraway seeds
> 1/2 teaspoon caraway seeds (optional)
> 1/2 medium white onion, halved and finely sliced
> 1/2 teaspoon ground turmeric
> 1 teaspoon wholegrain mustard
> 1 teaspoon Dijon mustard
> 2 tablespoons white wine vinegar
> 1 tablespoon white sugar

1. Preheat the oven to 190°C/fan 170°C/gas 5.

2. Use a small, sharp knife to cut through all the skin and tendons around the ankle of each duck leg. Press each duck leg bone towards the thigh as if holding pliers and cut through the tendon at the prominent leg-thigh joint. This helps the meat to relax when cooking. Rub a little sunflower oil into the duck legs and season with the dried thyme and 1 teaspoon of sea salt.

3. Put the duck legs on a small baking tray or in a small, ovenproof frying pan and place them into the oven for 1¼–1½ hours, or until they are crispy-skinned and the meat is totally tender to the push of a knife point.

4. Put the cucumber into a colander and mix in the remaining sea salt. Leave to drain over the sink for 30 minutes. When ready, wring out the cucumber with your hands to extract as much excess water as possible.

5. In the meantime tip the seeds into a small saucepan and jostle them around over a medium heat until a faintly toasted smell comes to the nose. Now add a dash of sunflower oil to the seeds, followed by the onion, and sweat over a medium heat for 3 minutes or so. Stir in the turmeric and cook for a further minute before adding the remaining ingredients. Simmer rapidly for 2 minutes, then transfer to a bowl and allow to cool.

6. When the vinaigrette is cool, add the cucumber and stir thoroughly. Leave to sit for at least 10 minutes.

7. Remove the duck from the oven.

8. Spread the cucumber over a serving plate and arrange the crispy duck legs on top.

Duck breast à l'orange

A classic for good reason – it is delicious. However, I veer more towards a rustic French recipe than to some of the over-orangey and sticky-sweet versions found in weird old country-house hotels that I've either discovered when filming or when I left wedding accommodation bookings to the last minute.

Serves 2

› 2 unwaxed oranges
› 1 thumb-sized piece of fresh ginger, peeled and finely grated
› 1 tablespoon plain flour
› 1 teaspoon flaked sea salt, plus extra for the dressing
› 2 large duck breasts, skin on
› a splash of sunflower oil
› 75ml red wine
› 1 dessertspoon dark runny honey
› 25g fridge-cold unsalted butter, cut into 4 pieces

To serve

› watercress, trimmed and washed
› walnut oil
› red wine vinegar or fresh lemon juice

1. Cut the ends off one of the oranges, then stand it on a board and cut off the rind in strips, vertically, all the way round, taking care to cut only the rind and not the white pith. Stack the slices 2 pieces high, roll them, then very thinly slice them.

2. Put the orange rind into a small saucepan and just cover with water. Bring to the boil and tip away the water. Repeat this stage, which will tenderize the peel. Drain and leave in the pan.

3. Squeeze the juice from both oranges into a small bowl and add the juice squeezed from the grated ginger.

4. Tip the flour on to a plate and add the sea salt.

5. With a sharp knife, score the duck skin in a close criss-cross pattern, taking care not to slash the meat.

6. Heat the sunflower oil in a small frying pan and, while it comes up to temperature, lower the duck breasts, skin-side down, into the seasoned flour. Lift them out and pat off any excess flour.

7. Lay the duck breasts skin-side down in the pan, where they should start to sizzle immediately. Turn down the heat to its absolute lowest. Cook them like this for 10–12 minutes. The sizzling should always be audible, gentle but steady, not spitting and mad and smoky, which will burn the skin.

8. When they are done on this side, turn the duck breasts over for a further 4 minutes, then remove them and lay them on a board, skin-side up. Leave them to rest somewhere warm. The skin should be irresistibly crisp. Resist! The meat should be pink within.

9. Put the frying pan back on the hob and turn up the heat. Pour in the wine and gingery orange juice and stir in the honey. Reduce rapidly by about two-thirds, or until syrupy. You should have only about 2–3 tablespoons of sauce.

10. Whisk in the butter, piece by piece, until the sauce is emulsified and glossy. Put the sauce to one side.

11. Slice each duck breast diagonally into about 6 pieces. It is easier to do this with the skin facing down, but turn the breast upright again immediately after carving.

12. Make sure that any juices on the board are whisked back into the sauce. Season the sauce further if need be.

13. Arrange the duck in the middle of your plates and spoon around the sauce. Serve with watercress, dressed with a little walnut oil, red wine vinegar or lemon juice and some sea salt. Some sautéed potatoes would be a fine accompaniment, too.

(Thai) beef salad

I am always reluctant to include the name of a country in a recipe title, in the same way that I always steer clear of the word 'authentic', unless I really know my onions, so to speak. I think it's prudent, as I have seen a lot of pan-global horrors called such things as Mexican chicken or Japanese spicy noodles, which would no doubt have the residents of said country weeping and beating the ground, howling with laughter.

I am no expert in Thai cooking, but my offering is both delicious and very refreshing and reminiscent of my Thai restaurant experiences. Concerning chillies, Thai dishes are often viciously hot, commonly inflicting pain and panic on the Western tongue. Please adjust the chilli presence as you see fit. I personally like the violence. If you have any rare roast beef left over from Sunday lunch, this is the perfect time to use it up.

Serves 4

> 1 teaspoon coriander seeds
> 2 teaspoons sunflower oil
> 350g good sirloin steak, or equivalent amount of rare meat left from the Sunday roast
> 1 medium cucumber, peeled, halved lengthways, deseeded and cut into 5mm slices
> 12 cherry tomatoes, halved
> 3 shallots, finely sliced
> 1 small gem lettuce, shredded, or a large handful of beansprouts
> 30g mixed fresh mint and basil, leaves picked
> 1 small red onion, halved and each half cut into 6 wedges
> 1 finger-length red chilli, very finely sliced on the diagonal
> flaked sea salt
> ground black pepper

For the dressing
> 3 tablespoons Thai fish sauce
> 1 tablespoon soft brown sugar
> 1½ tablespoons fresh lime juice
> 1 large clove of very good garlic, no green shoots, very finely minced
> 1 or 2 red or green bird's-eye chillies, very finely sliced

1. Dry-toast the coriander seeds, swirling the frying pan all the time until their fragrant smell comes to the nose and they start to pop. Transfer to a small plate.

2. Pour the sunflower oil into the frying pan and fry the steak on both sides until well coloured on the outside and rare within (2 minutes on each side). Season with sea salt and plenty of black pepper just before it is ready. Allow to rest for about 10 minutes.

3. Combine all the ingredients for the dressing in a bowl.

4. Slice the beef into thin strips and toss it together with the rest of the ingredients. Add any resting juices to the dressing along with the coriander seeds, mix well and toss together with the salad.

5. Eat with some ice-cold beers.

Good cheeseburger (and rules of engagement)

A good burger, I find, is not one found in artisan bread with homemade tomato chutney and extra mature Ticklebottom Farm Cheddar that doesn't melt properly. Onion in the meat is an ABSOLUTE NO-NO! Beaten egg to bind it is another ABSOLUTE NO-NO unless you actually want it to taste processed and rubbery. The point lies not just in the excellence of the meat but also in the plastic, techno-orange processed cheese, super-soft, crappy sesame bun and tomato ketchup. It must not be a crusty, crunchy tower that grazes the mouth and cannot be attacked unless you can dislocate your jaw like a snake. For a great burger there must remain the crucial element that is... JUNK.

P.S. Eat with French fries. None of that fat chip nonsense, please.

Serves 2

> 250g good fatty beef mince
> sunflower oil, for frying
> 2 pre-cut slices of weirdly orange processed cheese
> 2 sesame burger buns
> a leaf or so of iceberg lettuce per burger (very optional)
> 2 slices of beef tomato
> 2 thin slices from the middle of a red onion
> 1 large sweet pickled cucumber, sliced, for inside the bun, or 2 left whole for outside
> flaked sea salt

To serve

> ketchup
> mayonnaise

1. Form the mince into 2 burgers. Make them wide and flat, about 1.5–2cm thick, as opposed to high and dumpling-like. Do not season.

2. Get a pan hot over a medium heat and splash in a little sunflower oil. Put in the burgers – if the pan is hot enough, they should sizzle immediately. If the spitting sounds a little too enthusiastic, turn down the heat. Press them on to the metal a bit with your thumb or the back of a spatula. Cook for 2½–3 minutes. Before turning, season the raw side well with sea salt. Turn.

3. Lay the fake cheese over the cooked side and leave the burger to cook for a further 2½ minutes.

4. While the burgers sizzle, halve the buns and slot the halves into the toaster. Do not wait for the ejector to 'PLONG', as the bun wants to be only very lightly toasted... almost not. Plunge again if need be.

5. Place a lettuce leaf on the bottom half of each bun, or leave it out and start with the cheese burger, then layer with tomato, onion and sweet pickled cucumber (if using), finishing off with any squirty or smeary stuff. Alternatively, eat the sweet pickled cucumber whole, alongside the burger.

6. Load *Beverly Hills Cop* into the DVD player and eat the burger. Root beer (unfortunately hard to find) is a great accompaniment.

'For a great burger there must remain the crucial element that is... JUNK.'

Open burger on sourdough with onion gravy and fried egg

Although I love a burger in its most classic sense (*see* page 29), I don't eat all my burgers this way. Here's another hot favourite that's also good when made with venison mince. I first cooked this one gruelling rainy night after a harrowing drive to my sister's house from London, the last half hour a particularly distressing ordeal in trying not to squash a seemingly endless herd of frogs crossing the road. Below are the ingredients I found in my sister's fridge on arrival.

Serves 2

› 300g good fatty beef or venison mince
› 1 teaspoon flaked sea salt, plus extra for seasoning
› a hearty splash of Worcestershire sauce
› 2 teaspoons Dijon mustard, plus extra for the toast
› 1½ tablespoons sunflower oil
› 2 large free-range eggs
› 2 thick slices of sourdough bread, grilled or toasted
› softened unsalted butter, for spreading
› ground black pepper
› a handful of chopped chives, to garnish

For the gravy
› 1 medium onion, halved and finely sliced
› 30g unsalted butter
› ½ teaspoon demerara sugar
› ½ teaspoon tomato purée
› 2 teaspoons red wine vinegar
› 200ml canned beef consommé (freeze what's left)
› 100ml red wine

1. Squidge the mince, sea salt, Worcestershire sauce and mustard together in a bowl and form into 2 firm, flat, deep burger shapes.

2. Now start to make the gravy. In a pan fry the onion in the butter until very soft and turning golden brown. Add the sugar and caramelize even more before stirring in the tomato purée. Stir, but allow this to catch a bit on the pan before adding the red wine vinegar and cooking for a further minute or so.

3. Pour in the consommé and wine and simmer rapidly until the appearance of the gravy is only just syrupy rather than wet (this will take about 10 minutes), then season to taste and turn off the heat.

4. In a medium nonstick frying pan, heat the sunflower oil enough that the burgers sizzle on entry and cook them to your desired doneness (about 4 minutes or so on each side over a medium-high heat).

5. Rest the burgers, briefly, while you fry the eggs in the same pan and toast the bread. This would be a good time to reheat the sauce if need be.

6. Butter the toast, scrape over a little more mustard and place the burgers on their platforms. Spoon over the onion gravy, crown with the eggs, sprinkle over the chives and season with a scratch of sea salt and black pepper.

Hanger steak with cherry tomatoes

Hanger steak, as it's referred to by UK butchers, or onglet, as it's called in France, is a very delicious and flavoursome cut of meat, relatively unknown here and cheap too. Despite its deliciousness it does not respond well to overcooking – it must be cooked pink at least, otherwise it becomes tough – and must be cut across the grain to ensure tenderness. It's a cut I would not recommend to anyone who prefers their meat more towards grey than red.

This is great with fried garlic potatoes and salad dressed with walnut oil and lemon.

'Great with fried garlic potatoes and salad dressed with walnut oil and lemon.'

Serves 2

› 2 nice vines of cherry tomatoes, still attached to their stems, with 8–12 tomatoes on each vine
› 2 teaspoons olive oil, plus extra for drizzling
› 2 tablespoons red wine vinegar
› 400g hanger steak, trimmed
› 1 teaspoon dried rosemary
› 100ml white wine
› 15g bunch of fresh flat-leaf parsley, leaves chopped
› flaked sea salt
› ground black pepper

1. Preheat the oven to 220°C/fan 200°C/gas 7.

2. Put the cherry tomatoes, preferably still attached to their stems, in a small roasting tin or metal-handled frying pan. Drizzle with olive oil and scatter liberally with sea salt. Put into the oven for about 10 minutes, then splash in the red wine vinegar and return the tomatoes to the oven for another 5 minutes.

3. Get a small frying pan nice and hot. This is important, as the meat must brown quickly. Rub the steak generously all over with 2 teaspoons olive oil and season all over with sea salt, plenty of pepper and the dried rosemary.

4. Lay the steak in the pan; it should sizzle immediately. Turn it every now and then, having really given the steak a chance to pick up some colour so the meat is well browned. This will take around 5–6 minutes.

5. Transfer the steak to a board and allow it to rest for 5–10 minutes.

6. Gently slide the tomatoes and any cooking juices into the pan used to fry the steak. Add the wine and simmer over a high heat until the liquid has reduced to 3 or 4 tablespoons. Remove from the heat and stir in the parsley.

7. Slice the steak on the diagonal across the grain (go the other way and the meat will be tough and chewy). Divide between 2 warmed plates and top with the tomatoes and sauce.

Beef sirloin with my steak sauce

Midweek, if my spirits are flagging, I might resort to an invigorating kick-start from a piece of sirloin, cooked nice and rare. With it I like a good dollop of my own secret steak sauce. Not so secret now, I guess.

Serves 2

› 2 sirloin steaks
› unsalted butter or sunflower oil
› fried potatoes (optional)
› flaked sea salt

For the sauce
› 4 small gherkins, very finely diced
› 2 small shallots, very finely diced
› 2 tablespoons Henderson's relish or Worcestershire sauce
› 1 level teaspoon English mustard powder
› 2 tablespoons tomato ketchup
› 1/2 teaspoon ground black pepper
› 1 tablespoon finely chopped fresh curly or flat-leaf parsley
› 6 drops of Tabasco
› 1/4 teaspoon celery salt
› 1 free-range egg, hard-boiled, peeled and grated

1. Combine all the ingredients for the sauce in a bowl and mix them together thoroughly. Loosen with a tiny splash of water.

2. Get a frying pan nice and hot, add a little butter or sunflower oil and lay in the steaks – they should sizzle immediately. Season the side facing you with sea salt before flipping the steaks over.

3. Cook the steaks how you like them and serve with the sauce, accompanied by fried potatoes, if you like.

Rib of beef with artichokes and mushrooms

Just writing this recipe makes my mouth water. It's the kind of food I particularly like – uncomplicated, a simple delivery of true joy to the heart of the table. Rib of beef is not essential to the recipe, but I love cooking a single rib like a chop. For an excellent cheaper cut try hanger steak (see page 32). Often I will use freshly picked baby artichokes and different mushrooms such as chanterelles, blewits or ceps, but I've replaced them here with jarred artichokes and oyster mushrooms, as those are easier to find.

Serves 2

› 750g large single rib of beef
› olive oil or sunflower oil
› 285g jar of artichoke hearts in oil, well drained and cut into halves or quarters lengthways
› 150g oyster mushrooms or chanterelles, torn in half if bigger than your ear
› 2 cloves of good, hard garlic, with no green shoots (important as you are essentially eating it raw), very finely chopped
› a small sprig of fresh tarragon, leaves picked
› a small bunch of fresh curly parsley, very finely chopped
› juice of 1/2 lemon
› 2 tablespoons extra virgin olive oil
› flaked sea salt
› ground black pepper

1. Preheat the oven to 200°C/ fan 180°C/gas 6. Please feel free to cook the beef outside over charcoal if you wish, as woodsmoke, a wonderful ingredient in itself, will only make a good thing better. Otherwise, choose an ovenproof frying pan big enough to hold the rib, and get it nice and hot over a medium high heat.

2. Rub the rib all over with oil and season very generously on one side with plenty of sea salt and black pepper. Lay the seasoned side of the rib face down in the pan, where it should sizzle straight away. When it is well browned, turn the coloured side up and put the rib into the oven to finish to your preference, transferring it to a roasting tray if need be.

3. Once it's done, transfer the meat to a board to rest it, covering it with a little foil and a tea towel for 10 minutes or so.

4. While the rib rests, pour the dripping out of the pan and reserve it for cooking at a later date. Wipe out the pan (although the mushrooms and artichokes would be nice fried in the beef fat, it is not the taste I want). Put the pan back over a medium heat and tip in about a tablespoon more oil.

5. Add the artichokes and fry, tossing vigorously, until very well coloured. Now add the mushrooms and fry hard so that, by the time they are coloured, the artichokes are even more so.

6. Throw in the garlic and herbs and stir them through. Toss again with the lemon juice and make sure the seasoning is correct.

7. Serve the artichokes and mushrooms with the sliced beef, drizzled with the extra virgin olive oil.

Veal with mint and tomato

This just goes to show what delights can be cooked when people might be inclined to say, 'I just don't have the time' – a little cracker, thrown together one night to eat while writing this book, that was immediately written in once tasted.

Serves 2

> 400g British rose veal fillet
> 2 teaspoons plain flour
> 60g fridge-cold unsalted butter, cut into cubes
> 1 medium banana (long) shallot, halved and finely sliced
> 200ml good chicken stock
> 2 small cloves of very good garlic, sliced paper thin
> juice of 1/2 lemon
> 2 ripe medium tomatoes, skins removed, deseeded and finely diced
> flaked sea salt
> ground black pepper
> a small bunch of fresh mint, leaves roughly shredded, to garnish

1. Slice the veal into strips around 5mm wide. Season the flour well with a good pinch of sea salt and plenty of black pepper and toss the veal slices in it until evenly coated.

2. Heat 30g of the butter in a large, nonstick frying pan over a medium heat and fry the shallot for around 4–5 minutes, until softened. Remove from the pan and set aside.

3. Turn up the heat and add the veal. It should sizzle immediately on entering the pan. Jostle it around until lightly browned, turning every now and then. Return the shallot to the pan.

4. Gradually start to add the stock, stirring constantly until the sauce becomes smooth and has the consistency of single cream.

5. Throw in the garlic, lemon juice and tomatoes, stirring for just a few seconds, and remove from the heat. Stir the remaining butter into the sauce piece by piece.

6. Scatter over the mint and serve.

'A little cracker, thrown together one night to eat while writing this book.'

Veal Holstein

'Flippin' heck,' I thought when I first tried this brilliant feat of culinary engineering. I went back to the restaurant again that week just to check that I liked it as much as the first time. Although this dish of meat crowned with fried egg may appear butch, I assure you that the delicacy of the meat with the freshness of the lemon (the egg can always be jettisoned, I guess – although reluctantly) should prompt you to try it. It's more exciting than the savoury doughnut that is chicken Kiev.

Maybe this recipe will see some weep at feasting on one so young, as we in the UK still have not quite got our heads around eating veal. In the UK gone are the days of bull calves cramped in dark conditions (somewhat similar to my early years at boarding school). Now is the dawn of British rose veal where the calf receives a short but happy outdoor existence.

Serves 2

› 1 tablespoon plain flour
› 3 free-range eggs
› 1 tablespoon full-fat milk
› 75g pale fine dried breadcrumbs
› 2 × 150–175g British rose veal escalopes, beaten out to the thickness of 2 stacked £1 coins
› 75g unsalted butter
› 2 tablespoons olive oil
› 8 canned anchovy fillets, drained and roughly chopped
› 2 tablespoons baby capers, drained
› 15g bunch of fresh curly parsley, leaves finely chopped
› 2 tablespoons fresh lemon juice
› flaked sea salt
› ground black pepper

1. Scatter the flour over a plate and season well with sea salt and plenty of black pepper.

2. Beat one of the eggs with the milk in a bowl.

3. Spread the breadcrumbs out over a second plate.

4. Take one of the escalopes and coat it evenly in the seasoned flour. Then dip it into the beaten egg, dripping off any excess before you lay it in the breadcrumbs. Turn the escalope in the breadcrumbs until it is well coated. Set it aside on a plate while you prepare the second escalope.

5. Heat 25g of the butter with 1 tablespoon of the olive oil in a nonstick frying pan. When the fat is hot, add the escalopes to the pan and fry over a medium–high heat for 1½–2 minutes on each side, until golden brown and crisp.

6. While the escalopes are cooking, heat the remaining oil in a small frying pan and fry the remaining 2 eggs.

7. Remove the escalopes from the pan and transfer to 2 plates while you make the sauce.

8. Heat the remaining butter in a saucepan. (This could be done in the pan used to fry the escalopes, but it would need to be wiped out with a thick wad of kitchen paper first.) As it begins to foam, add the chopped anchovies, capers and parsley and sizzle for 30 seconds or so, stirring constantly. Stir in the lemon juice and remove the pan from the heat.

9. Top each escalope with a fried egg and spoon the sauce over.

Sausages and sauerkraut

What is British food? Fish and chips, pasties, pies and roasts is a tired old answer, and anyway our food culture has long been a hotch-potch of influences from visitors who waded on to our beaches clutching a sword or a basket of wares. Sauerkraut is cheap and delicious and very easy to find, be it in corner store, supermarket or Polskie Delikatesy. So try it. With the addition of smoked bacon, apples and onions, and accompanied by sausages, boiled potatoes and mustard, it makes for a real cold-weather feast – even more so if you decide to tip in a little cream. If you are without sausages it is also great coupled with a hot, thick, steaming slice of poached gammon (add a little of the stock to the kraut and leave out the bacon in this case). It is also surprisingly good with large pieces of white fish such as cod, haddock and bass.

Serves 6

› 12 fat garlic sausages, Toulouse or types of wiener
› sunflower oil, for rubbing
› 1kg small waxy potatoes, such as Charlotte, peeled (optional)
› 65g unsalted butter
› 1 large onion, halved and finely sliced
› 200g smoked streaky bacon lardons
› 2 bay leaves
› a little dried thyme or 1/2 teaspoon caraway seeds (optional)
› 6–8 juniper berries, slightly bashed
› 680g jar of sauerkraut
› 2 small Cox's apples, or similar sweet, tart and hard variety, peeled
› 100ml white wine (preferably a Riesling, as you can drink the rest with dinner)
› 150ml double cream (optional)
› flaked sea salt
› ground black pepper

1. Preheat the oven to 190°C/fan 170°C/gas 5.

2. Rub the sausages with a little oil and cook them in the oven until done. Alternatively, if they are wieners, poach them gently in hot water just before they are needed.

3. Meanwhile you can prepare the sauerkraut and, if doing boiled potatoes, now might be a good time to get the water on and peel them.

4. Melt the butter in a pan and sauté the onion with the lardons, herbs and other aromatics over a medium heat, stirring occasionally until deep golden but not browned (about 12 minutes).

5. While the onions are cooking, flop the sauerkraut into a colander and thoroughly rinse it under the tap. Gently squeeze out any excess water and add it to the onions when they are ready.

6. Grate in the apple on the large-holed setting of your grater. Add the wine and continue to cook the sauerkraut until the apple has softened and the wine has evaporated. Give the mixture a stir occasionally – it may begin to brown in places but this is okay.

7. Season the sauerkraut to taste, bearing in mind that it will take a little more sea salt than one may think, and adding a good grinding of black pepper. Add the cream, if you so desire, and stir through.

8. Spoon the warm sauerkraut into a serving dish, surround with boiled potatoes, if liked, and arrange the sausages over the top.

9. Eat immediately, with plenty of German or hot dog mustard such as French's and a bottle of cold wine such as Riesling.

Pork chops with cider cream sauce

I contributed this recipe to a book that never got published, so I took it back. Remember that, if you can't find a good perry, you can replace it with an interesting medium-sweet cider. This is delicious served with creamed celeriac and more perry or cider.

Serves 2

> 1 medium banana (long) shallot, finely sliced
> 1 clove of garlic, finely sliced
> 6 juniper berries, bruised with a pestle in a mortar
> 4 black peppercorns
> 2 sprigs of fresh thyme, plus extra to garnish
> 350ml good perry or cider (such as Burrow Hill)
> 75ml cider vinegar
> 1 teaspoon flaked sea salt, plus a little extra for seasoning
> 2 tablespoons plain flour
> 2 big fat pork chops
> 40g unsalted butter
> sunflower oil, for frying
> 50ml double cream

1. Preheat the oven to 200°C/fan 180°C/gas 6.

2. Put the shallot, garlic and aromatics into a small ovenproof frying pan. Pour over the perry or cider, along with the cider vinegar, and place over a medium heat. Reduce briskly until you have about a third of the liquid left, approximately 100ml (this will take around 12–14 minutes).

3. In the meantime, slide a knife right through the fat between the skin and meat of the pork chops at intervals 2cm apart.

4. When the reduction is done, strain it into a bowl and drop in the juniper berries picked from the wreckage.

5. Mix the salt with 1½ tablespoons of the flour and dredge the chops on both sides. Melt the butter in an ovenproof frying pan over a medium heat with a splash of sunflower oil to help prevent it burning. Fry the chops standing upright on their rind – they may need a little help (try to rest them against each other) for 4–5 minutes, or until relatively crisp.

6. Now lay the chops on one side to colour them richly for a further 1–2 minutes or so. Turn them on to the uncooked side and place the pan in the oven for 6–8 minutes. Ideally the pork should be faintly pink in the middle. You must judge it yourself, as chop sizes vary.

7. Once they are done, leave the chops to rest on a board for 5 minutes or so. Tip all but 1 tablespoon of the fat out of the pan. Return the pan to the hob and, over a low–medium heat, stir in the remaining flour for 20 seconds or so before pouring in the reduction. Stir well across the base of the pan in order to lift any tasty, coloured pork residue. Now pour in the cream and bring the sauce to a simmer. Season with extra sea salt, if necessary.

8. Spoon a generous amount of sauce on to 2 warm plates and place the chops on top, each garnished with a sprig of thyme.

Ibrahim's merguez

On the Golbourne Road in West London is a little stall outside the Oporto coffee shop. It's on wheels, but it hasn't really gone anywhere for years. Ibrahim, the owner, continues to serve great Moroccan food from this tiny space. What's more, it is one of the last great bargains to be found, as his prices seem not only to be cheap but have hardly risen in 11 years. Try the lentils, and the *baisara*... in fact, try everything.

Serves 4

› 16 merguez sausages
› 3 tablespoons extra virgin olive oil
› 2 tablespoons very finely chopped fresh coriander stalks
› 1 small red onion, coarsely grated
› 1 teaspoon ground cumin
› 1 teaspoon ground coriander
› 1 teaspoon ground black pepper
› 1 teaspoon ground ginger
› 2 cloves of garlic, finely grated
› 400g can of chopped tomatoes
› 100ml water
› fresh coriander leaves
› 1 teacup of couscous
› a sprinkling of ground cinnamon
› flaked sea salt
› harissa, to serve (*see* page 14)

1. Gently fry the merguez sausages in 1 tablespoon of the oil in a frying pan over a medium heat until just browned. Take care not to burn the sausages or the oil.

2. Remove the sausages from the pan and set aside. Add the coriander stalks to the oil, scrape in the onion and gently sauté for 8 minutes or so, again taking care not to burn them, until completely softened.

3. Stir in the spices and garlic and continue to cook the onions for another 2 minutes or so.

4. Add the tomatoes and water, then add the merguez and simmer gently for about 10 minutes.

5. Add the coriander leaves, season with sea salt and stir in 1 more tablespoon of the oil.

6. While the onions are cooking, put the couscous into a ceramic or Pyrex mixing bowl and rub in the remaining oil until all the grains are well coated.

7. Barely cover the couscous with boiling water. Place a tea towel over the bowl with 3 plates on top and leave for 10 minutes.

8. Remove the plates and cloth and fluff up the couscous with a fork.

9. Transfer the couscous to a serving bowl and dust it with cinnamon. Serve it alongside the hot merguez sauce, accompanied by my harissa.

Chorizo and potato flautas

A *flauta* (meaning a flute, so called because of its shape) is a tortilla shallow-fried with its filling snugly rolled inside. I'm crazy about tacos but sometimes, depending on the weather or my mood, by frying them in this way until crispy and golden, the *flautas* treatment just seems to make a good thing even better. This is a heavy hitter for cold autumn and winter days.

Although a Spanish chorizo is a markedly different thing from the Mexican version, it still makes a good replacement. You can buy proper corn tortillas, roughly 15cm in diameter, from the Cool Chile Company (www.coolchile.co.uk). Soft corn tortillas can be bought in most supermarkets but are not as authentic.

Serves 2-3

> 200g Maris Piper potatoes, cut into 1-cm dice
> 1 tablespoon sunflower oil, plus extra for shallow-frying
> 150g good fatty and soft cooking chorizo, diced
> 1 1/2 medium onions, diced
> 1 chipotle chilli, finely chopped
> 1/2 teaspoon ground cumin
> 1/2 teaspoon dried oregano
> juice of 1/2 lime
> 1 teaspoon flaked sea salt, plus extra to taste
> 6 soft medium corn tortillas
> ground black pepper

To serve

> fresh limes, for squeezing
> full-fat crème fraîche
> 2 tablespoons roughly chopped fresh coriander

1. Put the potatoes into a small saucepan and only just cover with water. Bring to a simmer, then cook for 8–10 minutes, until tender and crumbling around the edges. Drain and put to one side.

2. Heat the oil in a frying pan. Add the chorizo and fry gently for 1 minute, until it takes on some colour all over.

3. Add the onions and sauté over a medium–low heat for around 8 minutes until totally tender – add a splash of water if the pan begins to dry. Add the chilli, cumin, oregano, lime juice and sea salt and stir well.

4. Add the potatoes to the pan and cook for 1–2 minutes, until they are well coated in the oil. Season with more sea salt, if need be, and a good grind of black pepper. Remove from the heat and allow to cool slightly.

5. Set a large frying pan on the hob and bring it up to a medium heat. Gently warm the tortillas until they have softened (otherwise they will be difficult to roll without breaking). Use a tiny drip of sunflower oil in the pan and an occasional flick of water from the fingertips. Two can fit in the pan at the same time if they overlap.

6. Spoon some mixture into each tortilla and roll up, remembering that, although they want to be generously filled, they do need to roll with a considerable overlap.

7. Pour sunflower oil into the frying pan to a depth of roughly 5mm. Heat the pan over a medium–low heat, then, to test the temperature, take a piece of potato and drop it into the pan – it should just sizzle gently.

8. Working in batches, carefully place the filled tortillas in the pan, seam-side down, and cook until the seam sets in place. Cook for 6 minutes in all, turning them every 1 1/2 minutes. They should be deep golden and crispy all over.

9. Remove the *flautas* from the pan and serve with a squeeze of fresh lime, a dollop of crème fraîche and a little chopped coriander.

My 'not' Swedish meatballs

I rustled up this recipe for a 'Swedish meatball cook-off' that I filmed at a youth hostel. When I presented my entry to the judge, she told me that I had no right to call them Swedish meatballs.

I interjected that her comment was questionable, as here I was in Stockholm wearing an apron, after all. But the judge threw down her fork, turned up her nose and said, 'Unacceptable: they are too large and you have put dill in the sauce. What would my grandmother say? She would be appalled. Dill is for fish – you have broken a golden rule.'

Serves 4

› 100g unsalted butter, and maybe a bit more
› 3 medium banana (long) shallots, very, very finely chopped
› 400g British rose veal mince
› 400g fatty pork mince
› 50g stale white breadcrumbs (brioche is good, if available)
› 1 free-range egg, beaten
› 1/2 whole nutmeg, finely grated
› 2 teaspoons ground allspice
› 1/4 teaspoon ground white pepper
› 1–1 1/2 teaspoons flaked sea salt

For the sauce

› 2 1/2 tablespoons plain flour
› 125ml white wine
› 50ml white wine vinegar
› 500ml good beef or chicken stock
› 2 teaspoons caster sugar
› 1 tablespoon French's mustard
› 4 heaped tablespoons crème fraîche
› 3 tablespoons finely chopped fresh dill

To serve

› 4 large floury potatoes, boiled and riced
› cranberry or lingonberry sauce

1. Melt 50g of the butter in a small pan and sauté the shallots, stirring frequently, for at least 8–10 minutes, or until totally tender but not coloured.

2. Scrape the shallots into a large bowl and add the veal mince, pork mince, breadcrumbs and egg. Add the nutmeg and allspice, white pepper and a good amount of sea salt, remembering that the mince will need a considerable quantity more than you might normally put in. If you want to check your seasoning levels are correct, take a small amount of the mince and fry it in the shallot pan, give it a taste, then doctor the mince accordingly.

3. Really squeeze the mixture together, until completely combined, then fashion it into balls the size of a walnut in its shell.

4. Melt the remaining butter in a large frying pan and fry the meatballs carefully over a medium heat, turning regularly until golden brown all over, taking care not to burn the butter. The object is not to cook the meatballs completely, just to brown them. Remove the meatballs to a plate. Remove any stray bits of meatball from the butter with a slotted spoon.

5. To make the sauce, sprinkle the flour into the pan and stir it into the butter. Cook for about 30 seconds (do not burn the flour), then add the white wine and vinegar, stirring constantly for a minute or so. The flour will swell with the added liquid. Now follow with the stock. Simmer rapidly until the consistency of the sauce is similar to pouring double cream.

6. Stir in the sugar and mustard, then flop in the crème fraîche and swirl it in. Put the meatballs back into the sauce, bring the sauce to a very gentle simmer, put a lid on the pan and cook the meatballs for 5 minutes, checking that simmering hasn't turned into boiling.

7. Test the seasoning of the sauce one last time, then scatter over the dill and jiggle and stir it in.

8. Serve with the riced potatoes and accompany with large dollops of cranberry or lingonberry sauce.

Venison salad

I don't understand why we always view venison as autumn/winter meat and fit only for thick stews and heavy pies. We have six species roaming the UK wilds – the barking muntjac, pronking roe, elegant park fallow, regal red stag, fanged Chinese water deer and the sika – all with different seasons for male and female, meaning that there is deer to be eaten throughout the year. Certain cuts lend themselves well to the charcoal grill and salads, while also offering a delicious alternative to the normal Sunday roast joint. The mince makes a fabulous burger as well as rich pasta sauces. Here is a wonderful salad for the summer table.

Serves 2

› 1 tablespoon fresh thyme leaves
› 1½ teaspoons flaked sea salt, plus extra for seasoning
› 400g roe or fallow deer strip loin, trimmed of silvery sinew
› sunflower oil, for frying

For the dressing
› 20g unsalted butter
› 5 canned anchovies, drained
› 2 tablespoons Worcestershire sauce or Henderson's relish
› 2 tablespoons of the juice from a jar of pickled walnuts
› 1 teaspoon English mustard
› juice of 1 orange
› 1 teaspoon soft brown sugar
› ground black pepper

For the salad
› 10 whole fresh chives
› 1 tablespoon fresh tarragon leaves
› a few leaves of fresh lovage (optional)
› 2 big handfuls of pea shoots
› walnut oil, for dressing
› a little fresh lemon juice
› 4 cornichons, very finely diced
› 3 pickled walnuts, thinly sliced
› 1 medium banana (long) shallot, very finely sliced
› 6 hot French Breakfast radishes, cut in quarters lengthways
› a little grated fresh horseradish (optional)

1. Get a frying pan nice and hot over a medium heat.

2. Chop the thyme leaves with the sea salt. Season the venison fillet all over with this then rub the meat with a little sunflower oil and fry, turning the venison when need be so it has good deep colouring all around. Turn down the heat, add a little more oil to the pan and continue to fry the fillet, turning often, for approximately 8 minutes. Times will vary, as a roe loin is smaller than that of the fallow. Sizzling should be heard at all times, but not so fierce as to burn the meat or thyme. The loin should be cooked to very pink.

3. When the meat is done, rest it on a board where it will relax and become tender. Reserve any juices that run from the meat.

4. While the meat is resting, make the dressing. Heat the butter in the pan used to cook the meat. Drop in the anchovies and very gently sauté them for around 5 minutes, until totally disintegrated. Pour in the Worcestershire sauce or Henderson's relish and add the pickled walnut liquor, mustard, orange juice, reserved meat juices and sugar. Gently reduce until the dressing is just syrupy. Add a good grind of black pepper and allow the dressing to cool in a bowl.

5. When ready to serve, cut the chives in half and chuck them into a bowl with the herb leaves and pea shoots. Dress with a little walnut oil, lemon juice and sea salt.

6. Thinly slice the venison and lay it on a large plate. Scatter with a little crunchy sea salt. Flick over the venison with the walnut oil, thumb not totally covering the opening.

7. Sprinkle over the cornichons, pickled walnuts and shallot and place the radishes here and there in a random sort of way. Loosely arrange the pea shoots and herb salad over the meat, allowing them to fall freely and look buoyant.

8. Drizzle with the dressing, then grate over the horseradish lightly, if using, and serve immediately.

Venison mince with pearl barley

Wild venison is a much under-used meat and this is a shame, as we have plenty of it (*see* page 46). Annoyingly, the meat of all deer species is referred to as venison, making no clear distinction between the culinary merits of each. I feel indignant on behalf of the deer as a result. Suppliers and butchers need to label the meat properly. It is confusing for the customer who might try a red deer one week and a roe the next and would not necessarily understand why the taste was so varied over two occasions.

Near completing this book I was home alone, my wife helpfully staying away with her parents until I had crossed the finishing line. I was written off for the day – done in with writing – and cobbled the following together from the freezer, cupboards, vegetable basket and fridge. I got really into this recipe, deciding it should have the spicing elements of a great black pudding and the feel of a scooped-out haggis. The mince was from a deer I had shot locally, and all the wrinkly carrots, celery and parsley got used up – very satisfying. It's cheap in its origin and rich in its taste: the most pleasing combination. Despite really missing my wife and children, eating this with self-granted permission to watch Attenborough and *Avatar* instead of *Location* and *Lewis* was a rare treat.

Serves 6

› 75g unsalted butter, lard or dripping
› 3 medium carrots, quartered lengthways and medium diced
› 3 smallish celery sticks, finely sliced from end to end
› 2 medium onions, halved and finely diced
› 3 tablespoons finely chopped fresh parsley (stalks and leaves)
› 3 rashers of smoked streaky bacon, chopped to the same consistency as the mince
› 1 teaspoon dried thyme
› 2 bay leaves
› 4 cloves, crowns pinched
› a heavy grating of nutmeg
› 1 heaped tablespoon tomato purée
› 600g venison mince, from any of our six wild deer (*see* page 46)
› 100g pearl barley, rinsed
› 125ml red wine
› 1–1 1/2 teaspoons flaked sea salt
› ground black pepper

1. Melt the fat in a heavy casserole, one that has a lid. Add the carrots, celery, onions and most of the parsley and cook over a medium heat with the bacon, thyme, bay leaves, cloves, nutmeg and a heavy bombardment of black pepper. Stir often and, when the vegetables are softened and becoming tender, with only the faintest catching (not browning or burning) occurring, add the tomato purée.

2. Cook, stirring constantly, for another minute or so, then add the mince and cook, breaking it up all the time with a spoon to eradicate lumps. If it appears watery at first, continue to cook until that wateriness has gone, then stir in the pearl barley until evenly distributed throughout.

3. Stir in the wine and allow to simmer for a minute or so. Add enough water just to come up to the level of the mixture. Bring to a faint simmer, then regulate the heat to keep it that way, remembering that once the lid is on, the temperature will rise, so give it a check.

4. Cook, covered, for 40 minutes, checking once to see whether the mixture is moist enough to cook the barley. A little catching on the bottom of the pan is tasty, but don't confuse it with burning.

5. When done, the mixture should appear moist rather than wet or dry. Season with sea salt and stir in the remaining chopped parsley.

Dorset hot pot

This is just plain old cosy TV and blanket food for eating after coming home from walking the steep misty sheep tracks on the side of Lewesdon Hill, where my soul belongs.

Eat with buttered spring greens, cabbage, or cooked turnip or radish tops.

Serves 2

› 400g lamb neck fillet, sliced about 1.5cm thick
› 70g unsalted butter
› 3 rashers of smoked streaky bacon, roughly diced, or the equivalent amount of smoked streaky bacon lardons
› 1 large onion, halved and very thinly sliced
› a good scratch of mace or nutmeg
› a big pinch of dried thyme
› 1 bay leaf
› 1½ tablespoons cider vinegar
› 200ml good cider or water
› 200g waxy potatoes, skin left on and sliced 2mm thick across their width
› flaked sea salt
› ground black pepper

1. Preheat the oven to 210°C/fan 190°C/gas 6½.

2. Season the lamb pieces with a pinch of sea salt and plenty of black pepper. In a smallish ovenproof frying pan that will snugly fit the lamb, onion and bacon, heat 50g of the butter and fry the seasoned lamb briskly, taking care not to burn the butter, until browned all over.

3. Remove the lamb to a plate and add the bacon, onion, spice, thyme and bay leaf to the pan. Cook for around 10 minutes, or until tender. Do not rush or burn.

4. When the onion is ready, pour in the vinegar and evaporate it entirely. Nestle in the pieces of lamb and then pour over the cider or water. Remove the pan from the heat.

5. Starting with one in the middle, lay the potato slices on top of the lamb with substantial overlap to make sure you have enough potato to lambikins. Dot all over with the remaining butter and season the top with enough sea salt and black pepper to make the potatoes tasty in their own right.

6. Place in the oven with some tin foil over the top. Cook for 30 minutes, then remove the foil and brown for the next 20 minutes.

'This is just plain old cosy TV and blanket food.'

Lamb's liver

I don't understand how the UK's love of eating liver has faded in half a century – it's now seldom enjoyed, except by grandparents. It is so delicious with its mineral hit – invigorating! If you want to give it a try but don't want it served up grey with granule gravy, bacon, lumpy mash and a mug of tea (café style), here's how I cook it most often at home on the barbecue. I prefer to use metal skewers, as wooden ones can be problematic if placed over charcoal.

Serves 2

> 1 teaspoon ground cumin
> 1 teaspoon chipotle or regular chilli powder
> 1 teaspoon dried oregano
> 1 teaspoon flaked sea salt
> 1 clove of garlic, crushed
> 4 nice pieces of lamb's or pig's liver, sliced about 5mm thick
> 1 tablespoon sunflower oil or melted suet
> a little fresh lime juice
> 1/2 red onion, finely diced
> roughly chopped fresh coriander
> ground black pepper

1. Mix the cumin, chilli powder, oregano, sea salt, garlic and plenty of black pepper in a bowl. Add the liver to the bowl and turn it until well coated in the spices.

2. Thread the pieces of liver on to a metal skewer and paint with the oil or melted suet.

3. Place the skewers over the hot glowing embers of the barbecue. It is important that there are no orange flames. If flames flare up from any dripping fat, relocate the liver while the barbecue calms its temper. Cook the liver quickly over high heat close for about 2$1/2$ minutes on each side, until getting some good colour.

4. Remove the skewers to a plate, squeeze over some lime juice, then scatter over the red onion and some chopped coriander. Accompany with some cold lagers.

'Liver is so delicious with its mineral hit – invigorating!'

Kidneys in whisky sauce

Kidneys make the breakfast of champions, whether simply setting you up for the day or bolstering you against a hangover siege. In every sense a plate of kidneys is a welcome restorative, and I thank the lamb for its generous donation. I tend to eat this on rainy days that have to be spent outdoors with basket, gun, or hunched like a wet cormorant over my fishing rods.

The sauce is also excellent with Oloroso sherry and a bay leaf replacing the whisky and green peppercorns.

Serves 2

› 25g unsalted butter
› 75g very, very finely diced onion
› 1 tablespoon green peppercorns, plus 1¹/₂ tablespoons juice from the jar
› ¹/₂ tablespoon tomato purée
› 4 lamb's kidneys, skinned, cleaned and with core removed
› 3 rashers of smoked bacon, sliced into small batons
› 75ml Scotch whisky
› a wee pinch of ground cloves
› 100ml single cream
› flaked sea salt
› ground black pepper
› finely chopped fresh parsley, chervil or chives, to garnish

For the fried bread

› 2 slices of white bread
› sunflower oil
› a knob of unsalted butter

1. Turn on the oven to low and put in 2 plates to heat up. First make the fried bread, in a frying pan: gently fry the bread in oil and a little butter until golden and crispy while retaining a faint squidge. Drain on a plate lined with kitchen paper and put into the oven to keep warm.

2. Melt the butter in another frying pan and add the onion and peppercorns. Cook until the onion is totally soft and golden – do not hurry it on, however hungry you are. Add the tomato purée and stir in for a further 30 seconds or so. Meanwhile chop each kidney in half lengthways through the middle. Season generously.

3. Remove the onion from the pan to a plate and turn up the heat. Throw in the kidneys and bacon and fry them briskly but not so harshly that the butter burns. Jostle them every so often so that they colour evenly and, when they are nicely browned but weeping little pink juices, pour over the whisky and flame it (if you do not have gas, a lit match will help ignition, but stand back, as 7.30am is too early to lose your eyebrows).

4. When the flames calm down, return the onion to the pan, add the cloves and cook for a minute or so before adding the cream. Bring to a bubble and check the seasoning.

5. Serve with the fried bread, sprinkled with your chosen herbs.

'In every sense a plate of kidneys is a welcome restorative.'

Spicy cracked crab claws, Key style

This makes for very messy and enjoyable eating and is probably worth bibbing up for. A huge bowl of saucy claws was plonked on the table one Cornish weekend by my friends the Key family. A large group of us descended on it like a hunchbacked cackle of hyenas squabbling over the flimsy carcass of a zebra. To an onlooker the scene would have been quite shocking and the eating noises gruesome. The taste, however, was eye-rollingly delicious and when the frenzy was over, all disbanded from a gory, napkin-strewn tabletop with smeared and grinning lips. This is how I remember it, as no one could really recall the recipe when asked.

'This makes for very messy and enjoyable eating and is worth bibbing up for.'

Serves 2–4

› 1 teaspoon fennel seeds
› 1 teaspoon coriander seeds
› 1 tablespoon sunflower oil
› 1 tablespoon sesame oil
› 3 medium banana (long) shallots, very, very finely diced
› 1 tablespoon peeled and very finely chopped fresh ginger
› 4 cloves
› 4 star anise
› 1 1/2 teaspoons dried chilli flakes
› a 2.5cm strip of orange peel, cut with a potato peeler and twisted before hitting the pan to release the oils
› 5 cloves of garlic, very finely chopped, then smushed with the edge of a knife
› 1 1/2 teaspoons cracked black pepper
› 2 teaspoons Thai fish sauce
› 400ml kecap manis (Indonesian sweet soy sauce)
› 4 tablespoons tomato ketchup
› 12 large crab claws, raw or cooked
› 2 spring onions, finely chopped

1. In a wok or frying pan big enough to take all the claws and sauce, heat the seeds until just toasted. Swirl them often to prevent burning.

2. Add the oils. When they are on the verge of smoking, throw in the shallots, ginger, cloves and star anise and stir-fry, moving them constantly, for about 2 minutes, until the shallots are very tender. Add the chilli flakes, orange peel and garlic – again stirring all the time. Do not burn any of the ingredients. Turn down the heat.

3. Add the black pepper, fish sauce, kecap manis and tomato ketchup and stir in gently. Turn down the heat and simmer very slowly for 5 minutes or so.

4. Crack all the crab claws by folding them in a dish cloth and bashing them with something heavy. Do not use a wooden rolling pin, as you could dent the edge and it will stop rolling pastry well. Take care to crack the claws rather than to pulverize them to smithereens.

5. If using fresh, uncooked crab claws, drop them into the sauce and, when it comes up to a 'plup plup plup', continue to cook for 6 minutes. If using cooked crab claws, add them to the sauce for just 2 minutes, until you can be assured that the crabmeat within the shell will be hot.

6. Scatter with the spring onions then devour along with a cold beer.

Tuna tartare Barrafina

I very rarely eat tuna, but if I see a really firm, bright red piece of yellowfin I'll occasionally buy it and take it home, always for a raw or barely cooked treatment. This recipe is from Barrafina, one of my favourite places to eat in London. Nieves Barragán is the head chef and she has a head full of great ideas, which she executes with expert hands and serves to you on small plates. I always order this when I'm there.

Serves 4

› 2 teaspoons sesame seeds
› 320g super-fresh sustainable pole-and-line-caught tuna
› 8 dessertspoons Kikkoman soy sauce, preferably from a fresh bottle
› 4 dessertspoons sesame oil
› 4 dessertspoons good olive oil
› 2 teaspoons very, very finely chopped fresh chives

For the avocado purée

› 2 ripe Hass avocados
› juice of 1 medium lime
› juice of 1 small lemon
› 1/2 clove of good garlic, very very finely chopped then smushed with the side of a knife
› 30ml olive oil
› 15g fresh coriander leaves, finely chopped
› 3/4 teaspoon flaked sea salt

1. First make the avocado purée. Halve, stone and peel the avocados, then chop them roughly. Put them into a bowl with all the other purée ingredients and blitz with a stick blender until it's as velvety smooth as can be. Alternatively, this can be done in a jug blender. Put to one side.

2. Toast the sesame seeds by swirling them over heat in a dry frying pan continuously until golden. Tip them out and allow them to cool.

3. Slice the tuna into strips, then chop it very small. Use a sharp knife, and don't press on the fish too hard or you will make it mushy. Discard any sinewy little white strips that lie between the meat layers: they are as tough as dental floss. Place the tuna in a bowl.

4. Very gently stir the remaining ingredients into the tuna.

5. Gently press one-quarter of the tartare into a medium-sized pastry cutter, moulding it with the back of a spoon to give it a slight domed effect. Remove the mould and repeat three more times. Sprinkle the tartares with the sesame seeds.

6. Make 4 lovely quenelles of the avocado purée with 2 dessertspoons and set them down next to the fish.

Grilled squid with chermoula

Heavenly green sauce, charred tentacles, tender and giving flesh hissing and sizzling on the grill. When I am reminded of squid this way, I want it served up immediately. Remember that the squid should cook and colour very quickly so as to remain succulent. Make sure that the charcoals are properly hot – a hand held close to the grill should not be able to remain more than a second at most. You can also cook this indoors, on a cast-iron griddle pan. Get your fishmonger to prepare the squid if you'd rather not.

Serves 4

> › 4 medium squid with tentacles, opened and cleaned
> › 2 teaspoons coriander seeds
> › 2 teaspoons cumin seeds
> › 100g fresh coriander, stalks retained but roots cut off
> › 25g fresh mint, leaves picked
> › 3 large cloves of garlic
> › 1 teaspoon dried chilli flakes
> › juice of 1 lemon
> › 8 tablespoons olive oil
> › 1 1/2 teaspoons flaked sea salt
> › 1/2 small red onion, coarsely grated
> › lemon wedges, for squeezing

1. Lay the opened squid tubes on a board, inside facing up (to tell, you will notice that the outside looks a little shinier as opposed to the matt inside). Holding a sharp knife at a 45-degree angle, score the squid diagonally in parallel lines 5mm apart. Repeat in the opposite direction. Take special care not to cut all the way through the squid. Leave the tentacles and fins whole.

2. Toast the seeds in a dry frying pan. Tip them into a pestle and mortar and crush them lightly.

3. In a food processor or blender, blitz the fresh coriander and mint with the garlic, crushed spices, chilli flakes, lemon juice, oil and sea salt until well puréed. Transfer to a non-metallic bowl and then add the onion (blitzing it does strange things to its taste).

4. Put a quarter of the chermoula into a separate bowl and set aside. Add the squid to the rest of the chermoula and stir well until thoroughly combined. Cover the squid, chill and leave to marinate for 30 minutes.

5. Get your barbecue charcoal seriously hot but with all the flames gone – just whitish grey embers cracked with pulsing orange.

6. Place the squid bodies on the grill, scored-side down – they should sizzle immediately. Throw on the tentacles and fins.

7. Don't fidget the squid, just let the bodies get some good colour. If they do not roll up, just free the edges that may have stuck to the grill. Once they start to go they will roll up like a carpet curled from both ends. The tentacles and fins also want to be properly coloured, so attend to turning them when need be. Remember, charred patches on all the squid is GOOD.

8. Remove the squid to a plate and spoon over the reserved chermoula.

9. Serve the squid with lemon wedges for squeezing over.

Britta's salmon soup

This is one of the best fish soups I have ever eaten in my life, truly awesome. We arrived at the Tree House Hotel, outside Lulea in northern Sweden, exhausted, tired and smashed in from working in minus 35-degree temperatures and doing too much driving. Britta, the proprietor of this truly magical hotel, met us at the door, laughing, smiling and pouring out pure love from a jug of hot lingonberry juice into glasses. We felt instantly welcome and, having plonked our bags in our rooms, sat around a beautiful Swedish kitchen table to be served some incredible home cooking, starting with this soup. We went on to have reindeer stew, then a blueberry custard tart. I will never forget that meal. I hope you enjoy the soup as much as I did.

Swedish curry powder is mild but tastes rather different from our own. But just use whatever you can find; the results will still be pretty similar.

Serves 6

› 50g unsalted butter
› 1 medium leek, finely sliced
› 2 celery sticks, finely sliced
› 1 good tablespoon mild curry powder
› 400g can of chopped tomatoes
› 1 fish stock cube
› 400ml just-boiled water
› 500g salmon fillet, skin off and chopped into large chunks (about 4cm)
› 600ml double cream
› flaked sea salt
› ground black pepper

1. Melt the butter in a large saucepan and sauté the leek and celery for about 10 minutes, until the celery is soft and the leek is taking on some colour. Add the curry powder when the vegetables are noticeably becoming softer and continue to cook for a minute or so, stirring frequently.

2. Flop in the tomatoes and cook for about 5 minutes, to get rid of the initial tinny taste. Dissolve the fish stock cube in the just-boiled water and pour into the saucepan. Bring up to a gentle simmer and cook for 2 minutes or so.

3. Drop in the salmon and cook for 6 minutes, stirring occasionally. If it overcooks slightly or breaks up when stirred, don't worry.

4. Pour in the cream, bring to a gentle simmer and bring out the taste with sea salt if necessary (it will take more than you think) and a generous grind of black pepper.

'This is one of the best fish soups I have ever eaten in my life, truly awesome.'

Tom yum talay

I don't cook a lot of Thai food. I like eating it, certainly, but I feel I don't have enough understanding of the basics, yet, to include much more of this cuisine in my book. (I need some lessons!) However, this is my favourite Thai soup, and I have had a few discussions with Thai restaurateurs about how this bowl of eye-wateringly hot, sharp, aromatic, fishy joy should be assembled. Were you to find me eating this alone, as I always seem to, the tears pouring from my eyes would suggest I had received some tragic news. Don't worry, it's the chilli. Thai food takes no prisoners when it comes to heat. Most supermarkets now stock a fair few Thai ingredients and your local oriental one certainly will. Galangal, lemon grass and lime leaves will freeze well for next time. There may be lot of ingredients but the soup can be made in half an hour flat.

Serves 4

> 1¹/₂ tablespoons sunflower oil
> 2 cloves of garlic, very finely sliced
> 2 medium banana (long) shallots, finely sliced
> 1 tablespoon finely chopped fresh coriander stalks, plus a handful of leaves
> 4 green or red (or a mix) of bird's-eye chillies, roughly chopped
> 6 kaffir lime leaves
> 1 large thumb-sized piece of fresh galangal, washed and thinly sliced
> 2 stems of lemon grass, outer sheath removed, cut into 1cm slices on the diagonal
> 1 teaspoon shrimp paste
> 2 teaspoons soft light brown or palm sugar
> 3 tablespoons fresh lime juice
> 900ml good chicken stock, tasty but not too strong or dark
> 1 tomato, core removed, cut into quarters
> 4 closed-cap or chestnut mushrooms, cut into quarters
> 2 tablespoons Thai fish sauce
> 12 environmentally acceptable raw tiger or king prawns, peeled
> 300g big mussels, debearded
> 2 medium squid with tentacles, cleaned, body cut into ¹/₂cm rings or slices, tentacle clusters halved

1. Heat the oil in a large saucepan. Add the garlic, shallots, coriander stalks, chillies, lime leaves, galangal and lemon grass and fry for 2 minutes, stirring constantly so as to prevent them from burning.

2. Tip the shrimp paste into the pan, add the sugar and lime juice, then stir well and add the stock and tomato. Bring the stock to a simmer, stir in the mushrooms and fish sauce and simmer for 3 minutes.

3. Drop the prawns into the liquid, return it to a simmer and cook for 1 minute. Add the mussels (discarding any that are open and don't close when you tap them) and the squid and cook for a further 2 minutes or until the mussel shells have opened (throw away any that don't).

4. Divide the broth between 4 bowls, making sure that there is an even distribution of fish. It is customary to serve up the shards of lemon grass and other aromatics and eat your way around them. Scatter with a handful of coriander leaves.

5. Serve immediately, with a box of paper napkins for the tears.

Rudimentary fish soup

This recipe shows just how simple a fish soup can be and how quickly it can be prepared. In fact, this is just the kind of thing I've often made on a boat with only the bare essentials. There are times when fish stock is called for, but remember, if there is enough fish meat to water, there is your flavoursome stock. I made this when filming, and it went down a storm after we nearly went down in a storm.

Serves 4

> 3 tablespoons olive oil
> 1 medium leek, thinly sliced into 5mm rounds
> 1 medium bulb of fennel, halved and medium diced (taking off the outer layer is often unnecessary; remove it only if stringy)
> 2 fresh bay leaves
> 1 teaspoon fennel seeds
> 6 black peppercorns
> 1/2 teaspoon dried rosemary
> 2 cloves of good garlic, very finely sliced
> 200ml dry white wine
> 1.2 litres water
> 2 teaspoons flaked sea salt
> 400g Maris Piper potatoes, peeled and diced a little smaller than mouthful size
> 500g sea bass, bream, gurnard, cod, or a mixture, filleted, skinned and cut into large pieces
> 3 tablespoons chopped fresh parsley
> good crusty bread, to serve

For the garlic mayonnaise

> 8 tablespoons shop-bought mayonnaise, such as Hellmann's
> 1 teaspoon Dijon mustard
> 1 free-range egg yolk
> 2 tablespoons good olive oil
> a small squeeze of fresh lemon juice
> 3 cloves of good hard garlic, chopped and smushed with a little flaked sea salt

1. Pour the olive oil into a large pan or soup pot, then put it over a medium heat and sweat the leek with the fennel, bay leaves, fennel seeds, peppercorns and rosemary for 10 minutes or so, stirring often, until nearly tender. Stir in the garlic and cook for a further 2 minutes.

2. Add the wine and bring to the boil for 3 minutes or so before adding the water, sea salt and potatoes. Bring the soup back to a simmer and cook for about 10 minutes, until the potatoes are only a fraction less than ready (try one).

3. While the potatoes are cooking, make the garlic mayonnaise. Put the mayonnaise, mustard and egg yolk into a bowl and mix together. Beat in the olive oil with a fork and drip in a little lemon juice to give it an edge. Stir in the garlic and put to one side. If you want to make the mayonnaise from scratch, then do so, but food cooked on windy beaches or in boats calls for a clever cheat now and then.

4. Drop the fish into the soup and jostle it under the water by shaking the pan a bit. Once it is simmering again I would propose cooking it for a mere 2–4 minutes, so that the fish is only just done. Add the parsley to the soup.

5. Ladle into bowls and stir in a large spoonful of the garlic mayonnaise.

6. Eat with good crusty bread.

Turmeric sardines in tomato sauce

Golden fish on a small red sea bring Sinbad the sailor to mind – only momentarily, though, as this thought is going nowhere. Delicious and just the kind of thing I seek out for a simple lunch or dinner.

Serves 2

- › ½ tablespoon ground turmeric
- › 2 tablespoons plain flour or chickpea flour
- › 1 teaspoon flaked sea salt
- › 4 plump sardines, scaled, gutted and patted dry with kitchen paper
- › 4 tablespoons extra virgin olive oil
- › warmed white rolls, to serve

For the tomato sauce

- › 2 tablespoons extra virgin olive oil
- › 1 small clove of garlic, finely minced
- › 2 tablespoons finely chopped fresh coriander leaves
- › a good pinch of ground cinnamon, to taste but not to overpower
- › ½ teaspoon ground coriander
- › ½ teaspoon ground cumin
- › ½ teaspoon cayenne pepper
- › 200g tinned chopped tomatoes
- › ½ teaspoon caster sugar
- › juice of ¼ small lemon, to give an edge but not to overpower
- › ½ teaspoon flaked sea salt

1. For the tomato sauce, heat 1 tablespoon of the oil in a small saucepan and gently sauté the garlic with the fresh coriander and dried spices for 1 minute, stirring constantly. The garlic must not brown or the spices burn.

2. Flop in the chopped tomatoes, adjust the heat and gently simmer for 5 minutes or so, stirring the mixture occasionally. The sauce wants to be loose and sloppy but not watery.

3. Stir in the sugar and tweak to taste with the lemon juice and sea salt. Stir in the remaining oil, then remove from the hob and gently reheat when needed.

4. Now for the sardines. Mix the turmeric, flour and sea salt on a plate and roll the fish in it until well coated.

5. Heat the oil in a large frying pan, taking care not to burn it. Place the sardines side by side in the pan, where they should start to sizzle immediately. Cook for 2–3 minutes on each side – the skin should be crisp and have a rich golden colour.

6. Spoon the warmed sauce over the middle of 2 plates and lay 2 golden fish upon each.

7. Eat with warm white rolls in the North African way.

Fritto misto with cheat's aioli

Fritto misto, or mixed fry as it translates from the Italian, used to feature regularly on the menu at Alastair Little's. I was constantly frying myself bits and bobs throughout service given half a chance, which would result in emergency fish filleting and another caution. Quite simply, it's battered fish, but the sage leaves, aioli and lemon just make it a special thing. If you want to make the aioli from scratch, see the recipe for Grilled Quails with Almond Mayonnaise on page 23 but omit the almonds.

Serves 2

> sunflower oil, for deep-frying
> 200g fillets of gurnard, red mullet, gilthead or black bream, cleaned of scales (the skin can also be removed from the bream or gurnard, if desired)
> 6 large fresh sage leaves
> 4 small sprigs of celery leaves, rinsed and totally dried (fresh flat-leaf parsley would be good too)
> lemon halves, to serve

For the cheat's aioli

> 1 free-range egg yolk
> 4 tablespoons shop-bought mayonnaise, such as Hellmann's
> a generous glug of good olive oil (about 2 tablespoons)
> 2 fat cloves of garlic, very finely chopped or minced
> a squeeze of fresh lemon juice, to taste

For the batter

> 330ml bottle of light lager, such as Peroni Nastro Azzuro, fridge-cold
> 200g Doves Farm gluten and wheat free self-raising flour, plus an extra tablespoon for dusting
> flaked sea salt

1. First make the aioli. Beat the egg yolk into the mayonnaise, then beat in the olive oil until you can just begin to taste it. Stir in the garlic and squeeze in enough lemon juice so that you know it's there but it doesn't steal the show.

2. Heat the sunflower oil to 180°C in a deep-fryer or medium saucepan.

3. Make the batter by pouring only just enough beer into the flour so that, when they are briefly mixed together, it is a little thicker than good pouring double cream. It must not come dribbling off once the fish is dipped into and lifted out of the batter. Leave to stand for 5 minutes or so, adding a good pinch of sea salt just before you start frying.

4. Make sure that the fish fillets are totally dry. This is essential in order for the batter to stick to the fish. Divide each fillet diagonally into 3 pieces.

5. Dust a plate with the tablespoon of flour and roll the fillets in it until evenly coated. Pat off any excess flour clinging to the fish. Dip them in the batter and drop them into the oil. Fry for 2–3 minutes, turning once. When done, the fish pieces should be crisp and golden. Drain on kitchen paper.

6. Dip the sage and celery leaves directly into the batter, flick off any excess and deep-fry for 30 seconds or so, until crisp. Drain likewise.

7. Serve with the cheat's aioli and lemon halves, for squeezing.

Fish curry

India has offered up some of the best fish dishes I have ever eaten – amazing prawn and sweet sticky shrimp birianis, tandooried butterfish and curried crab, to name but a few. Mmm! My recipe is hot, so add only as much of the chilli as you see fit.

› 70g ghee or unsalted butter
› 1 medium onion, halved and grated
› 1 large fresh bay leaf
› 3 cloves of garlic, finely chopped
› 1 thumb-sized piece of fresh ginger, peeled and very finely chopped
› 3 green bird's-eye chillies, trimmed and finely chopped (or leave whole for a mild curry)
› 1 teaspoon ground turmeric
› 1/2 teaspoon ground cumin
› 1 teaspoon garam masala
› 1 1/2 tablespoons tomato purée
› 1 teaspoon caster sugar
› 1/2 tablespoon tamarind paste
› 200ml coconut water (not milk) – from the cold-drinks section of the supermarket
› 1/2 teaspoon flaked sea salt
› 300g fish fillets, such as gurnard, bream, bass or mackerel, cut into large chunks
› a small squeeze of fresh lemon juice
› 2 tablespoons double cream (optional)
› a small handful of fresh coriander leaves, roughly chopped, to garnish

1. Melt the ghee or butter in a frying pan or wok and very gently sauté the onion with the bay leaf for 10 minutes or so, or until deep golden and totally tender. Add the garlic, ginger and chillies, stirring them around enthusiastically for little more than a minute.

2. Add all the spice powders and stir them around for no more than a minute, so as not to burn them. Add the tomato purée and sugar and cook for a further minute, stirring often.

3. Dilute the tamarind with the coconut water and pour into the curry, then bring to a simmer for 2 minutes or so. Season generously with the sea salt. You must get this dead on to counteract the sourness from the tamarind.

4. Slip the fish into the sauce and cook for 4–5 minutes. Don't stir the fish around once cooked, otherwise you will break it up. Jiggle or gently swirl in the lemon juice. This can be followed with a swirl of double cream, if desired.

5. Serve with plenty of chopped coriander scattered over the top.

Killer fish tacos

I love fish tacos in all their forms, but this one is gloriously full-on, in that the fish is not only battered and deep-fried but also lounges on a tortilla, to be smeared in chipotle mayonnaise – equivalent to an oiled-up dude lying on a beach towel. This is hardcore dirty eating at its most enjoyable. Whiting is an unpopular fish and this is unfortunate, as it is plentiful, cheap and very delicious, especially when deep-fried. I'd say cats have got the edge on us. Give it a go.

Sometimes 2 tortillas are stacked on top of each other per serving, as this taco can get quite juicy – in which case buy double the number of tortillas.

Makes 6

> 75g white cabbage
> 1/2 large ripe Hass avocado
> sunflower oil, for deep-frying
> 6–12 corn tortillas
> 250–300g whiting, cod, bream, hake or gurnard fillet, skinned and cut on the diagonal into slices 10–12cm long and 2.5cm wide
> flaked sea salt

For the salsa

> 1 large vine tomato, finely diced
> 1/2 small red onion, finely diced
> juice of 1/2 lime
> 1/2 teaspoon flaked sea salt
> 1/4 teaspoon dried oregano
> 1 teaspoon sunflower oil
> 1 tablespoon finely chopped fresh coriander, stalks and all

For the chipotle mayonnaise

> 5 tablespoons shop-bought mayonnaise, such as Hellmann's
> 3 teaspoons chipotle paste
> 1 teaspoon tomato ketchup

For the batter

> 200g Doves Farm gluten and wheat free self-raising flour
> 270ml cold lager

1. Combine everything for the salsa in a bowl and put to one side. Combine everything for the mayonnaise in a bowl and put to one side.

2. Combine the batter ingredients and allow to stand for 4–5 minutes.

3. Shred the cabbage very finely. Halve, stone and peel the avocado and slice it into sixths lengthways. Line a plate with sheets of kitchen paper, ready to drain the fish on.

4. Heat the oil to 180°C in your deep-fryer or heat up a medium pan with enough oil to shallow fry.

5. Put your largest frying pan on the hob and bring it up to a medium heat. Start warming the tortillas through with a tiniest drip of sunflower oil in the pan and an occasional flick of water from the fingertips. Two can fit in the pan at the same time if they overlap: just rotate them occasionally. They should go from card-like and stiff to limp and delicious-smelling. Store in a tea towel.

6. Keep on with your tortilla-warming while you fry the fish. In 1 or 2 batches, dunk the fish in the batter and fry, turning once, until deep golden. Drain on the kitchen paper and season with a little sea salt.

7. When ready, take a tortilla (stack 2 if desired). Place a little cabbage along the middle and a slice of avocado on top. Season with a tiny pinch of sea salt. Lay the fish on top. Blob with a good dollop of the mayo. Top with the salsa.

8. Gather up each side and EAT WITH YOUR FINGERS.

9. This goes well with 1/4 lime juice to 3/4 cold lager, poured into a salt-rimmed glass.

Clams with jamón and sherry

I have a serious appetite when it comes to clams. Give me one plate and I'll order another. This is probably my favourite way to eat them, a very popular dish from Spain. It reminds me of little restaurants you may find in side streets. Those hot afternoons, one arm dangling over the back of a wooden chair, wilting with the combination of cold beer and hot sun, with that wonderful feeling of no hurry. Lots of little plates, scrumpled-up paper napkins and a crumb-strewn table – all the signs of a good lunch. Happy days!

Please do not be put off by the flour in the recipe – you can simply leave it out if you like and enjoy the dish with an unthickened sauce.

Feel free to replace the jamón with smoked bacon, since if all you can get hold of is the sliced stuff it's a bit extravagant. Most Spanish delis sell offcuts from cured ham legs.

Serves 2

› 700g fresh clams
› 50g unsalted butter or 50ml olive oil
› 1/2 medium onion, finely diced
› 50g offcuts of Jamón Iberico, sliced thinnish and cut to roughly the same shape as a postage stamp (use sliced jamón if offcuts are unavailable)
› 2 bay leaves
› 2 medium cloves of garlic, very, very finely sliced
› a splash of sherry vinegar (optional)
› 1 1/2 teaspoons plain flour (optional)
› 50ml Oloroso or Amontillado sherry
› a handful of roughly chopped fresh parsley
› ground black pepper
› flaked sea salt (optional)

1. Put the clams into a colander and shake them about very vigorously under fast-running cold water, as this should break apart any that were filled with silt and prevent the dish from being sabotaged. Discard any clams that are open and don't close when you tap them.

2. Over a medium heat melt the butter or heat the oil in a frying pan that has a lid and is big enough to happily accommodate the clams. Throw in the onion, ham and bay leaves and sauté them until the onion is tender, whilst taking care not to burn them or the butter. This will take about 8 minutes.

3. Grind in some black pepper and follow with the garlic, then stir everything together for 30 seconds or so. Sprinkle over a good splash of sherry vinegar (if using) and allow it to evaporate.

4. Add the flour, if using, and stir it in for a further minute or so, taking particular care not to let it brown. Pour in the sherry, then stir in the clams and cover the pan with the lid. Jiggle everything around briefly.

5. Steam the clams for 3–4 minutes, or until only just opened. Remove the lid and stir in the parsley. The sauce should have thickened. Check the seasoning and add sea salt if you think it is needed, then serve immediately, picking out and discarding any clams that remain closed as you come across them.

Oysters Rockefeller

This recipe is only an approximation of a classic, as its inventor, Jules Alciatore, took the combination of ingredients to the grave with him, or so it is said. Oddly enough, some knowledge prevails that the inclusion of spinach is a 'no-no'. Is the recipe a secret or not?

Mine does include spinach, and what's more you can of course pass the recipe on to whomever you see fit. The ingredients list is long but the preparation time short. The results are well worth it.

Serves 6

› 1 medium banana (long) shallot, very finely chopped
› 2 medium celery sticks, plus a few leaves if any, very finely chopped
› 1 clove of garlic, finely grated
› 125g unsalted butter
› 2 tablespoons Pernod
› 1 tablespoon small capers, or chopped large ones
› 8 small cornichons, finely chopped
› 150g fresh spinach, cooked, then well pressed and drained and allowed to cool
› 1/3 bag of watercress
› 1/2 teaspoon flaked sea salt
› 2 tablespoons fresh tarragon leaves
› 1/2 teaspoon fennel seeds
› 1 heaped teaspoon Dijon mustard
› grated zest of 1/2 large unwaxed lemon and a small squeeze of fresh lemon juice
› 12 very large rock oysters, opened and released but with each oyster left in its half shell
› lemon wedges, to serve (optional)

For the breadcrumb topping

› a large handful of good coarse dry breadcrumbs
› 1 1/2 tablespoons extra virgin olive oil
› 1 1/2 tablespoons grated Parmesan cheese
› ground black pepper

1. Preheat the oven to 220°C/ fan 200°C/gas 7.

2. Sweat the shallot, celery and garlic in a third of the butter until totally softened but not coloured – about 10 minutes in all. Add the garlic near the end so as to ensure you do not burn it.

3. Pour in the Pernod and bubble until evaporated. Stir in the capers and cornichons and cook for a further minute. Allow to cool.

4. Put the shallot mixture into a food processor with the spinach, watercress, sea salt, tarragon, fennel seeds and mustard and blend, dropping in knobs of the remaining butter as you go. The blended mixture should be semi-smooth.

5. Add the lemon zest, then squeeze in just enough juice to give the mixture a faint sharpness rather than overpower it. Stir through.

6. Now prepare the breadcrumb topping. Put the breadcrumbs in a bowl and add the olive oil and Parmesan. Grind in a lot of black pepper and mix together. Set aside.

7. Top each oyster with a generous spoonful of the green butter and a sprinkling of the breadcrumb topping. Place on a baking tray and bake in the oven for about 5 minutes, or until just bubbling and the crumbs are browned.

8. Serve with lemon wedges, if liked.

Lobster cocktail

The combination of smoky chipotle chilli and shellfish is a wondrous thing. I appreciate that lobster is expensive, but occasionally I want to push the boat out. This recipe is also prompted by having a few fishermen friends with lobster pots who eat so much lobster that they like to have it in different ways in order to avoid boredom.

This Mexican-style cocktail is a winner and also very good with crab or octopus. You may find the use of pineapple weird, but let me tell you, it takes the whole cocktail from something good to something great... that is, if you like pineapple.

Chipotles are smoke-dried jalapeño chillies that need rehydrating before you use them. The cooking time below can be shortened if the chipotle is already rehydrated or you use chipotle paste from a jar (this can be bought in good supermarkets). I tend to keep a batch of rehydrated chipotles in the fridge, as I use them a lot at home.

Serves 4

› 700–800g fresh, live lobster
› 1 tablespoon sunflower oil
› 1 big clove of garlic, finely chopped
› 1 small ripe Hass avocado
› 1/2 medium red onion, finely diced
› 2 very ripe tomatoes, medium diced
› 100g slice of fresh pineapple, peeled and medium diced
› 1 fat green chilli (not bird's-eye) or 1/2 jalapeño chilli, finely diced

› a small bunch of fresh coriander, leaves coarsely chopped, stalks very finely chopped
› ground black pepper
› lime slices, to garnish

For the dressing
› juice of 1/2 orange
› 4 tablespoons tomato ketchup
› 1 generous teaspoon Worcestershire sauce
› a small pinch of ground cloves (be careful, as too much could overpower the whole dish)
› 1 big chipotle chilli, deseeded and rehydrated in a little just-boiled water, then drained, chopped and mashed to a paste, or the equivalent amount of chipotle paste
› juice of 2 small juicy limes
› 1/2 teaspoon dried oregano

1. Combine all the ingredients for the dressing and put it into the fridge immediately to chill, as it is best served refreshingly cold.

2. Lower the lobster into rapidly boiling water and, once it is boiling again, cook for 7 minutes. Remove from the water and allow to cool.

3. When the lobster is cool, break off the head, taking care to catch any watery juices. The creamy brown stuff should be mixed into the dressing.

4. Cut down the length of the body through the middle and prise out the fresh meat. Green goo is okay, don't freak: just wipe it away from the head

end of the meat. Chop the meat into large chunks. Break the claws, extract all the meat and divide it into large chunks. Reserve any juices for later.

5. Pour the oil into a frying pan and get it very hot. Only then throw in the lobster pieces and fry very hard and quickly, until quite golden brown. If the pan is not hot enough and the lobster does not sizzle immediately, by the time it colours the meat will be overcooked. Stir in the garlic for 30 seconds or so, then pour in any reserved juices from the lobster.

6. Evaporate the liquid fast, until reduced and sticking to the pan. Stir the lobster and syrupy juice together, then immediately tip on to a plate. Allow to cool.

7. Halve, stone and peel the avocado and cut the flesh to the size of board-game dice. Put the onion, avocado, tomatoes, pineapple, green chilli and coriander into a nice serving bowl. Add the lobster and gently combine everything together.

8. Pour over the chilled dressing and toss lightly together, taking care not to mash the ingredients, until they are well coated. Add a good grind of coarse black pepper.

9. Garnish with slices of lime and eat with corn tortilla chips, forks and an unending supply of tequila.

Devilled prawns

I first encountered this in Colombo, Sri Lanka. I had been very ill in India, and in order to recover I checked into a nice hotel. Pale and wasted, tucked up in bed, I got on to room service and ordered devilled prawns – a Sri Lankan speciality. I made a speedy recovery on at least one plate a day while reading an inexhaustible stash of trashy novels I found in the hotel lobby. Sometimes when I discover a new dish it's all I want to eat.

I like all the shell peeled from the prawns – when eating in some Thai or Indian restaurants, it's very aggravating to have a forkful interrupted with the necessity to stick your fingers into your mouth to remove the tail. A pleasurable eating experience marred.

The hopper is a sour little coconut milk pancake popular in Sri Lanka that is excellent with this dish. I have not learnt to make them yet, so rice will have to suffice.

Please regulate the chilli heat as you see fit, as I like the devil wicked.

If the cooking time seems short, that's because the vegetables are meant to be only par-cooked.

Serves 2

› 4 tablespoons sunflower or groundnut oil
› 1 medium red onion, halved and sliced about 3mm thick
› 1 small thumb-sized piece of fresh ginger, peeled and very finely chopped
› 1/2 stick of cinnamon, broken in half
› 2 cloves of garlic, finely minced
› 1 teaspoon hot red chilli powder
› 2 fresh hot green chillies, chopped
› 16 curry leaves (optional)
› 250g raw tiger prawns from a sustainable source, peeled and deveined (thawed if frozen)
› 1 teaspoon ground turmeric
› 2 medium vine tomatoes, one cut into sixths, one roughly chopped
› 1 green pepper, deseeded and finely diced
› 1 teaspoon flaked sea salt
› 2 tablespoons tomato ketchup or tomato purée
› a squeeze of fresh lime juice
› steamed rice, to serve

1. Have all your ingredients ready to go as the prawns must be cooked only briefly in the wok or frying pan. All the cooking should be done within 3–4 minutes so the prawns don't overcook.

2. Heat the oil in the pan so that when things are thrown in they sizzle vigorously and immediately.

3. Add the onion, ginger, cinnamon and garlic, followed by the chilli powder, fresh chillies and curry leaves. Toss together, frying for barely more than 30 seconds and taking care not to burn the garlic.

4. Now add the prawns, followed by the turmeric. Stir vigorously, then, after about 20 seconds, add the tomatoes and green pepper and season with the sea salt. Toss or stir often for the next 3 minutes.

5. Add the tomato ketchup or purée and the lime juice and cook for a further 10 seconds or so.

6. Check the seasoning, divide the prawns between 2 warmed plates or bowls and eat with steamed rice.

Simple baked lobster

This may seem complicated but is not, and is a luxurious treat of treats. Great served with watercress and a good bottle of chilled Chablis.

Serves 2 as a starter or 1 as a main course

› 550–600g fresh, live lobster
› 1 medium banana (long) shallot, very finely chopped
› 40g unsalted butter
› 3 tablespoons brandy
› 1 tablespoon plain flour
› 150ml fresh or ready-made fish stock
› 75ml double cream
› 2 teaspoons Dijon mustard
› 1 teaspoon tomato purée
› 1 tablespoon finely chopped fresh tarragon
› a squeeze of fresh lemon juice
› 25g Gruyère or Parmesan cheese, finely grated
› flaked sea salt
› ground black pepper
› watercress, to serve

1. Bring a pan of well-salted water up to the boil and carefully drop in the lobster. Bring back to the boil and cook for 6 minutes. The lobster is only partly cooked at this point, as it will be cooked more under the grill. Remove from the water with tongs, put on a board and allow to start cooling.

2. In the meantime, sauté the shallot gently in the butter for 8 minutes or so, until totally softened but only very lightly coloured.

3. Add 2 tablespoons of the brandy and flame it (if you do not have gas, a lit match will help ignition). Reduce to around 1 tablespoon. Scatter in the flour and, stirring constantly, cook for a further 30 seconds or so, taking care not to burn it.

4. Slowly add the fish stock, stirring all the time so that you obtain a creamy consistency with no lumps. Simmer the sauce gently for 2–3 minutes, stirring constantly until thickened.

5. Add the cream, followed by the mustard and tomato purée, and cook until the sauce has the consistency of thick custard. Stir in the remaining brandy. Stir in the chopped tarragon, followed by just enough lemon juice to give the sauce an edge rather than overpower it. Season to taste with sea salt and pepper.

6. Preheat the grill to high, with the oven shelf set two shelves away from the element.

7. Trying to keep the claws attached to the lobster, wrap each claw, in turn, with a tea towel and hit it just hard enough to crack the shell without bashing it to smithereens.

8. Split the lobster in half lengthways with a large sharp knife. Start by pushing the point into the lobster's head. The job will take two cuts.

9. Remove any dark green bits from the head cavity. Do not scrape out the remaining creamy insides, as they are delicious. Place the lobster halves in a shallow ovenproof dish or on a rack above a grill pan, cut-side up. Remove the tail meat, chop into chunks, then return it to the shell.

10. Spoon the sauce over the lobster meat, all the way along the length of the lobster, then scatter the cheese over the top.

11. Place the lobster under the grill and cook for 4–5 minutes, until browned and bubbling.

12. Serve immediately with watercress alongside.

Deep-fried scallops, Japanese style (hotate fry)

This might strike you as downright weird, but the accompaniments to this dish, although Japanese, are a fruit sauce almost indistinguishable from HP (tonkatsu sauce), and English mustard. It's odd, but it works, and here is the recipe.

Panko is a Japanese type of flaked breadcrumb that is readily available in most large supermarkets. You may be interested to know that these breadcrumbs come from bread baked using an electric current rather than heat: electrocuted breadcrumbs!

Serves 2

> sunflower oil, for deep-frying
> 3 tablespoons HP sauce
> 1½ teaspoons Japanese soy sauce
> 2 tablespoons plain flour
> 1½ teaspoons flaked sea salt
> 2 free-range eggs
> 75g panko breadcrumbs
> 12 large king scallops, no corals (roe), preferably from the shell and prepared in front of your eyes by a fishmonger (if you don't know how)

To serve
> ¹/4 small white cabbage, shredded
> lemon wedges
> English mustard

1. Heat the oil to 170°C in a deep-fryer or medium saucepan.

2. Mix the HP sauce and soy sauce together in a bowl and set aside.

3. Scatter the flour over a large plate and add the sea salt. Beat the eggs in a bowl. Put the breadcrumbs into a separate bowl.

4. Dry the scallops thoroughly with kitchen paper, then roll them in the seasoned flour until evenly coated. Dip each coated scallop into the beaten egg until it has a generous covering, then roll the scallop into the breadcrumbs until well coated.

5. Deep-fry the scallops in batches until golden brown.

6. Serve with the shredded cabbage, lemon wedges, some English mustard and the sauce to dip into.

'The accompaniments, although Japanese, are a fruit sauce almost indistinguishable from HP, and English mustard.'

Scallops with garlic cardamom butter and curry leaves

Simplicity itself, this is a cracking dish and has become one of my absolute favourites. Ideally the scallops would be coupled with a cold bottle of good, crisp white wine, condensation running down the side, and eaten in a warm breeze coming off the twinkling sea, the salt air mingling with the smell of the scallops and curried butter. Damn! I'm still here writing this in the office on a cold Sunday.

The scallops must be very, very good, preferably fresh from the shell. Wretched, long pre-picked victims in a watery tub are better left alone.

Always remember to remove the belt from around the main white scallop muscle as, left on, it will constrict while cooking and cause the scallop to be chewy. Eat or leave the corals (roe) as you prefer.

Serves 4 as a starter or 2 as a main course

› 1 medium bulb of good hard garlic
› 100g unsalted butter
› 12 fresh (ideally) or dried curry leaves
› seeds from 10 cardamom pods, ground fairly finely in a pestle and mortar or equivalent set-up
› 1/2 teaspoon ground turmeric
› 1/4 teaspoon dried chilli flakes (optional)
› about 1/2 teaspoon flaked sea salt, plus extra for seasoning
› sunflower or vegetable oil, for dipping the scallops
› 8 super-fresh large fat king scallops, preferably from and including the shell, cleaned, with coral kept or discarded according to preference, skirts removed and discarded
› lime wedges, to serve (optional)

1. Preheat the oven to 220°C/fan 200°C/gas 7.

2. Roast the garlic for 30 minutes, or until the flesh is very soft and beginning to colour golden brown. Allow to cool a bit, then skin all the garlic cloves, leaving just the soft roasted flesh.

3. Melt the butter in a small frying pan and, when it is hot but not smoking, throw in the curry leaves and cardamom. The curry leaves should spit and pop. Fry, stirring constantly, for a good 30 seconds or so.

4. Add all the garlic flesh and the turmeric and mash it into the butter.

5. Allow to sauté gently for a further 2 minutes or so while you add the chilli flakes (if using) and sea salt to taste. Be careful not to let the garlic burn. If the butter has gone a faint nut brown, this is fine. When the butter is done, leave to one side.

6. Put a small frying pan over a high heat and get it very hot. Pour a little sunflower or vegetable oil on a plate and dip both flat sides of each scallop before lowering them into the pan. (This should be done to the coral too, if using.) An aggressive sizzling should be heard the minute the scallops kiss the pan. This hard fry will caramelize the plentiful sugars in the scallop meat, creating that heavenly savoury toffee.

7. Turn the scallops (and corals, if using) after about 1–1 1/2 minutes, or after one side is browned, and brown the other side for a further minute. The middle of the scallop should remain almost raw. Warm the curried garlic butter now, if need be.

8. Season the scallops with a little extra sea salt and arrange them either back in their shells or on a plate.

9. Spoon over the warmed garlic butter and serve with wedges of lime, if desired.

Finger-licking shrimps

Varying combinations of garlic, some sweetness and tomato, dusted over with smoky chillies, always deliver. It's a kind of swanky barbecue-saucy affair that can be thrown together in minutes. Summer outdoors food.

Serves 2–4

› 100g unsalted butter
› 1 medium onion, finely chopped
› 4 fat cloves of garlic, finely chopped
› a pinch of ground cloves
› 2 good teaspoons chipotle chilli powder or paste
› 2 tablespoons tomato purée
› 150ml sweet sherry
› juice of 1/2 lemon
› 1 tablespoon olive oil
› 500g sustainable raw whole tiger prawns or other jumbo shrimp, heads removed but tails left intact
› a good handful of fresh parsley, roughly chopped
› flaked sea salt
› lemon slices, to garnish

1. Melt the butter in a saucepan and gently sauté the onion for about 12–15 minutes, until meltingly soft and certainly golden but not brown.

2. Add the garlic for the last couple of minutes, stirring regularly until the garlic is tender but not burnt. Add the cloves and chipotle chilli powder or paste, stirring for around 30 seconds.

3. Flop in the tomato purée and cook until it starts to catch and colour slightly. Stir all the time to help prevent the onions, garlic and spices from burning. Pour in the sherry and reduce until the mixture appears quite creamy. Squeeze in the lemon juice.

4. Pour the oil into another pan and, when hot but not smoking, throw in the prawns and fry quite hard for around 1 1/2 minutes, until their shells are really quite coloured.

5. Tip the sauce into the pan with the prawns and stir through briefly until the sauce is hot. Remove from the heat and stir in the parsley.

6. Taste the sauce and add a little sea salt. Garnish with lemon slices and eat with good bread and cold beers.

Bagna càuda

If you don't really like anchovies or garlic, avert your eyes, as this recipe will horrify you. If you do like these things, then this is a heavenly, creamy sauce in which to bathe the vegetables and eggs... or maybe even yourself! The garlic must be excellent. This recipe was kindly given to me after a heavy grappa session with Mitch Tonks.

The vegetables below are my preferred suggestion, but please replace as you see fit.

Serves 4–6

› 2 medium bulbs of good hard garlic (no green centres or shoots)
› a small sprig of fresh rosemary
› enough extra virgin olive oil to cover the garlic (not the really expensive stuff)
› 3 × 50g cans of salted anchovies in olive oil, drained
› 50g cold unsalted butter, cubed, to finish
› lemon wedges, for squeezing

For the vegetables

› 2 good red peppers, deseeded and cut into sixths lengthways
› 1/2 small cauliflower, leaves and main stalk removed and head broken into florets
› 2 endives, stem base removed and split into sixths lengthways
› 12 baby carrots, cleaned and topped, tailed if necessary
› 6 baby beetroots, cooked until tender, then peeled and halved
› a bowlful of Ratte, Enya or other salad potatoes, cooked until tender and left to cool
› 6 free-range eggs, hard-boiled, peeled and halved

1. Break up the garlic bulbs, cut off any hard ends, then skin all the cloves and put them into a small pan (otherwise you will use far too much olive oil) with the rosemary. Just cover the garlic with olive oil.

2. Over a low heat, bring the oil up to no more than a bare wobble and cook the garlic until 100 per cent softened and nothing less. It must not brown, however. This will take about 20 minutes.

3. Pour off approximately a quarter of the oil and keep it for cooking something else. Discard the rosemary stalk but don't worry about any leaves that have become separated from it. Put the pan back over a low heat.

4. Put in the anchovies and cook until they have totally collapsed.

5. Take the saucepan off the heat and whiz in the cold butter, using a stick blender – the mixture will become creamy.

6. Serve the sauce while it is still hot, in a warmed bowl on a wooden board surrounded by the vegetables and eggs.

7. A squeeze of lemon on the veg before they enter the bagna càuda is very nice. *Bene!*

Mackerel with passion fruit salsa

My friend Joe came across this after filming in Brazil. He told me the story of a man in a battered hat behind his stall on a coastal road, leaning over a tiny barbecue as he knocked up this salsa in seconds to then pour it over a charred and sizzling piece of fish. I went home and cooked it immediately, knowing it would be delicious – and it was! I can imagine that the sauce would also work well with thin slices of raw fish, marinated like a ceviche.

If you cook the fish over charcoal, make sure it is wiped totally dry first and heavily scattered with some good flaked sea salt, as this should prevent it sticking. Ideally a barbecue would be better than a grill, as charcoal smoke is a magic ingredient.

Serves 2

› 2 medium mackerel, gutted and wiped as dry as possible
› flaked sea salt (approx. 1/2 teaspoon for each fish)
› lime wedges, to serve

For the passion fruit salsa

› 1/2 hot green chilli, such as jalapeño or serrano, seeds scooped out, very finely diced
› 3 fat and full passion fruit, flesh and seeds scooped out
› 1 tablespoon olive oil
› juice of 1/2 small juicy lime
› 2 tablespoons very finely chopped fresh coriander, stalks and all
› 2 tablespoons very finely diced red onion
› flaked sea salt

1. Preheat the grill to high.

2. Slash the mackerel three times down each side, and season well with a good amount of sea salt, probably more than you would normally be inclined to use.

3. Lay the fish on the grill and place them not too far from the element. Cook for approximately 4 minutes on each side, or until the skin is blistered and browned, taking care not to rip the delicious skin when turning them over. The mackerel should be cooked, but ever so reluctant to pull from the bone without a bit of prompting. If the flesh is just cooked but with a red blood line running along the spine, you have done it perfectly.

4. While the fish blister, make the passion fruit salsa. Combine all the ingredients in a small bowl and season well with sea salt, tasting a few times.

5. Remove the fish to 2 plates and spoon over the salsa.

6. Serve with lime wedges and eat accompanied by cold beer drunk from the bottle, not a glass.

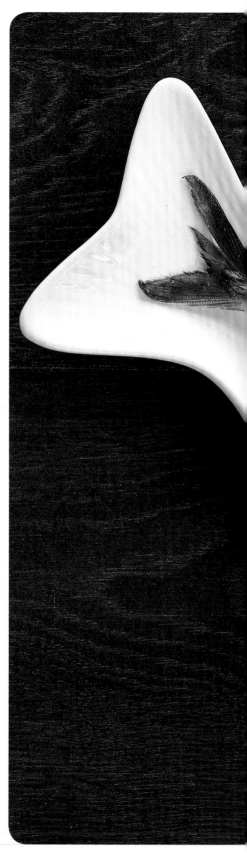

Mackerel with passion fruit salsa

'Serve with lime wedges and eat accompanied by cold beer drunk from the bottle.'

Bream with fennel

If you get the chance, buy a black bream, a more common cousin of the gilthead bream that is also found in our waters or farmed and imported from abroad. The meat is firm and most excellent, and I think superior to the gilthead. Fennel and fish – nothing new here, just one of those great marriages. The dressing brings a lively freshness, a little dance, to the dish. But if you don't want to make the dressing, leave it out – the fish and fennel with a wedge of lemon are a fine thing on their own. Likewise, eat the fish without fennel and add the dressing to a small gem lettuce, cut in six wedges lengthways, replacing the fennel tops with mint.

Serves 2

› 1 teaspoon fennel seeds
› 40g unsalted butter
› 2 medium bulbs of fennel, green tops and fronds removed, roughly chopped and reserved, flesh chopped into small chunks
› 4 cloves of garlic, halved
› 1 small glass of water
› 1 small glass of white wine
› 75ml full-fat milk
› olive oil, for frying the fish
› 1 tablespoon plain flour (optional)
› 1 medium gilthead or black bream, filleted
› flaked sea salt
› ground black pepper

For the dressing

› 1 tablespoon pine nuts
› 2 tablespoons extra virgin olive oil, plus extra for frying
› 5 canned anchovies, drained
› 1 large lemon
› a little pinch of dried chilli

1. Place a saucepan over heat and toast the fennel seeds until their smell comes to the nose, then add the butter. Add the fennel and garlic and sauté until beginning to soften but not colour. Add the water and wine, then simmer with an offset lid for 15 minutes, or until the fennel is totally tender and the wine has evaporated. The wine must be totally cooked away so it does not split the milk when you add it.

2. Pour in the milk, then turn down the heat and very gently simmer, stirring often, until the consistency is creamy and soft. Season with sea salt and black pepper.

3. While the fennel cooks, make the dressing. Toast the pine nuts by swirling them over a low–medium heat in a frying pan that is large enough to take the fish fillets later on. They should be golden brown when done. Tip them into a bowl.

4. Pour some oil into the pan and fry the anchovies until they collapse. Scrape them into the pine nuts and add the reserved green fennel tops and fronds.

5. Cut both ends off the lemon and stand it on a board, then cut off the rind, pith and inner skin of half of it. Cut out 4 segments of flesh, slice each into little pieces and add to the bowl. Add the dried chilli. Add the 2 tablespoons olive oil and set aside.

6. Wipe out the frying pan, add a little more oil and and reheat it.

7. If flouring, place the fish fillets, skin-side down only, in some seasoned flour scattered on to a plate. Pat off the excess. Lay the fillets in the pan, skin-side down. On entering the pan the fillets should sizzle immediately, but make sure the heat it is not so fierce that they burn.

8. Place a side plate on top of the fillets to stop them arching up and help crisp the skin. Put the fennel back over a gentle heat.

9. After 3–4 minutes, remove the little plate and check the fish. When you have two fingers' width of uncooked flesh running down the centre of the fillets, flip them over and turn off the heat. Leave them there for 30 seconds.

10. Spoon some fennel on to the centre of each plate and put the crispy-skinned bream on top. Spoon some of the dressing over the skin and serve.

Poached trout with lentil salad

I fish for trout a lot and like to enjoy them in many different ways in order to avoid boredom. That, I guess, is seasonal cooking anyway. This is so easy to make and could be done by the riverside while fishing or camping, although I'd probably make the lentils at home. If you do cook the fish outdoors, poach it and experience the wonderful effect of preparing it 'au bleu'. Drop a small, simply gutted and de-gilled trout that you have only just before knocked on the head into simmering water to which a splash of vinegar has been added. The protective slime that coats the fish's body will turn blue when slipped into the hot water to cook. Charming magic.

Serves 2

› 100g Puy lentils
› 500ml cold water
› 1 slice of wholemeal bread, cut to the size of board-game dice
› a good glug of olive oil
› 500g rainbow or brown trout, cleaned and de-gilled
› 4 tablespoons finely chopped fresh parsley leaves (reserve the stalks for the court bouillon)
› 1 tablespoon chopped fresh tarragon leaves
› 2 tablespoons chopped fresh mint
› a splash of fresh lemon juice
› flaked sea salt
› ground black pepper

For the court bouillon

› 100ml white wine
› 1/2 small onion, roughly sliced
› 1 celery stick, roughly chopped
› 1/2 sprig of fresh rosemary
› 1 sprig of fresh thyme
› a few stalks from the parsley
› 6 black peppercorns
› 1 large bay leaf
› 2 tablespoons vinegar
› 500ml water

For the vinaigrette

› 1 1/2 generous teaspoons Dijon mustard
› 1 tablespoon red wine vinegar
› 1 small clove of good garlic, finely grated
› just under 1 teaspoon caster sugar
› 50ml olive oil, plus extra for the croûtons
› 1/2 teaspoon flaked sea salt

1. Put everything for the court bouillon into a pan big enough to fit the trout. Bring it up to a very low simmer with the lid on.

2. Put the lentils into another pan and cover them with the water. Bring them to the boil, then turn them down to a simmer and cook for approximately 30 minutes, or until they are tender. Make sure they are not too bitey, but neither should they resemble anything too mushy.

3. While the lentils cook, make the vinaigrette. Mix the mustard, vinegar, garlic and sugar, then beat in the olive oil. Season with the sea salt.

4. Drain the lentils, season delicately with sea salt and a good grind of black pepper, then leave to one side to come to room temperature.

5. In a small pan, heat the oil and fry the cubes of bread until golden and crispy, then drain on kitchen paper.

6. Bring the court bouillon up to the boil. Lay the trout in the pan and bring the liquid back to a simmer. Cook it gently for 6–8 minutes, then remove from the pan to a plate and allow it to cool a little. Peel the skin away and slide the meat from the bone with a knife, trying to keep it intact.

7. Mix the vinaigrette into the lentils, followed by the herbs. The salad should be nice and moist, but loosen with a bit more olive oil if necessary. Sharpen with a little fresh lemon juice.

8. Spoon the lentils on to the centre of 2 plates and sprinkle over a few of the croûtons.

9. Lay a trout fillet on top of each lentil salad. Cold cider would be a good accompaniment.

Grilled trout with hazelnuts and horseradish

Someone once sent me an angry email saying I was a fool to extol the virtues of foraging, as didn't I realize people are too busy to have time to go out and pick their dinner after a long day at work. I replied that he appeared to have missed the point. Isn't it better to know when you just happen to be standing next to a hazelnut bush, rather than not?

This is an ideal little meal for when camping, hopefully beside a twinkling, gurgling, sunlit stream teeming with plump, freckled brown trout.

This is very good eaten with watercress. If you are lucky enough to find it wild near to where you are camping, even better, but make sure you wash it well in at least two changes of salty water.

Serves 2

> › 40g unsalted butter
> › a handful of hazelnuts, thinly sliced (they will break a little, but this doesn't matter)
> › 500g rainbow or brown trout, cleaned, de-gilled and wiped totally dry
> › 1 clove of garlic, very, very finely chopped
> › a small handful of fresh chives, finely chopped
> › a small handful of fresh curly parsley, finely chopped
> › grated zest of 1/4 small unwaxed lemon and a squeeze of juice, just enough to give the sauce an edge
> › a thumb-sized piece of fresh horseradish root
> › flaked sea salt
> › watercress, to serve

1. Put a small frying pan on the barbecue and in it melt the butter. Throw in the hazelnuts when it is foaming, taking care not to burn it. Gently cook the nuts until a rich golden colour, swirling them often and regulating the heat should the butter be colouring too fast. Put aside on a warm area of the grill.

2. Before putting the trout on the barbecue, make sure the coals are grey with a healthy orange glow showing through. Also make sure the trout is wiped totally dry (wet fish on a hot grill will guarantee it sticks fast).

3. Very generously cover the trout with some sea salt. Not only does this season the fish but it also helps lift the skin slightly from the bars, preventing the fish from sticking.

4. Cook the fish for approximately 3–4 minutes on each side or thereabouts – it wants to be only just cooked close to the bone. Cook the trout close enough to the heat that the skin gets crisp and browned. Transfer the fish to a plate.

5. Drop the garlic into the pan of hazelnut butter and stir in the chopped herbs. Finally add the lemon zest, then squeeze enough juice into the butter to give it a nice twang while not being too sharp.

6. Spoon the herb and hazelnut butter over the trout and then grate fresh horseradish over the top of your fish. Serve with watercress.

Citrus-marinated sea bass with charred spring onions

I made this for a photo shoot in winter on a South African beach, where the day before a fishing boat had been overturned and washed up, sadly with one hand lost. It was still there, upside down. Strewn about lay some of the uncollected catch, with most of these fish missing chunks from shark bites. The wind whipped my legs with sand and shivered the dense, low bushes, while huge waves surged and pounded this expanse of golden sand under a cold sun. It was one of the most beautiful places I have ever been, while at the same time wild, desolate and melancholic.

We prepared this behind the protective thicket, using a fish known as cob. It was delicious and sat next to a plate of gazelle tartare I'd also prepared. Sea bass is quite similar to cob, but both bream and gurnard would also be very good.

Serves 4

› ¹/₂ teaspoon cumin seeds
› 8 black peppercorns
› 4 cloves, bashed
› 2 fresh bay leaves, crumpled
› 125ml freshly squeezed sweet, tart orange juice
› 2 tablespoons red wine vinegar
› 1 long, fleshy hot green chilli or ¹/₂ Scotch bonnet chilli, finely sliced
› 500g sea bass, bream or gurnard, filleted, pin-boned and skinned, then sliced on a long, shallow diagonal into thin slivers
› 6 sprigs of fresh young thyme
› ¹/₂ teaspoon flaked sea salt
› 4 tablespoons olive oil
› 6 spring onions

1. In a small saucepan, dry-toast the cumin seeds with the peppercorns and cloves, swirling them often. Take them to the point just before they start to burn and their toasted smell comes strongly to the nose.

2. Drop in the bay leaves, then pour in the orange juice followed by the vinegar. (This way round and you are less likely to be gassed by the vinegar.)

3. Drop in the chilli slices. Bring the mixture to a simmer, then take off the heat and allow to cool completely.

4. Lay the fish pieces, only slightly overlapping, across the bottom of a platter, then fold, crumple and strew over the thyme. Scatter over with the sea salt.

5. Pour the infused citrus marinade over the fish, followed by 3 tablespoons of the oil, and leave to marinate for 30 minutes.

6. While the fish marinates, trim the spring onions, if necessary, and rub them with the remaining oil.

7. Get a small frying pan or griddle pan very hot and lay on the onions in a row. Cook for 4–5 minutes or so, turning occasionally. They want to be very charred, so cook them for longer if need be.

8. Serve the fish with the charred spring onions laid on top.

White fish with parsley sauce and bacon

If I were a plate of food, this is what I would be. A truly comforting dinner for when the rain is hitting the window panes while a brave few are out at sea.

Parsley sauce should be green, not pallid with green flecks. I would also add that flat-leaf parsley gets too much press these days. I'd always use curly parsley here, as I prefer its gentler taste and softer leaf. Bacon is great with parsley sauce, parsley sauce is great with white fish, and white fish is great with bacon. Circle of joy, using the best of British.

Serves 2

› 40g unsalted butter
› 4 rashers of smoked streaky bacon
› 1/2 teaspoon flaked sea salt
› 1 tablespoon plain flour
› 2 big thick shoulder or mid-fillet pieces of cod, pollack or coley, approx. 170g each (skin left on)

For the parsley sauce

› 20g unsalted butter
› 15g plain flour
› 250ml full-fat milk
› 20g mature Cheddar cheese, grated
› 1 good teaspoon wholegrain mustard
› a grating of nutmeg
› 2 tablespoons double cream
› 5–6 tablespoons very, very finely chopped fresh curly parsley
› flaked sea salt
› ground black pepper

1. Preheat the oven to 220°C/fan 200°C/gas 7.

2. To make the parsley sauce, melt the butter in a small saucepan and stir in the flour. Cook out the dry taste of the flour for 30 seconds, stirring occasionally, taking care not to burn it. Then start adding the milk, bit by bit, until you have stirred it into a smooth sauce whose texture resembles that of double cream.

3. Stir in the Cheddar, mustard and nutmeg and simmer gently for 5 minutes, stirring regularly, then add the cream. If the sauce seems a little thick, add a splash more milk, or reduce it if it seems a little thin. It should have a consistency only a little thicker than pouring double cream. No more, no less. Season to taste with sea salt and pepper.

4. In a frying pan, melt the butter over a medium heat and get the bacon frying.

5. Mix the sea salt with the flour and press the fish fillets into this, skin-side down (do not flour the flesh side). Pat off any excess flour. Lower the fillets into the pan, skin-side down, and fry for about 5 minutes, or until the skin is browned and crispy, taking care to turn the bacon.

6. You may have had to remove the bacon from the frying pan by now if it is getting close to burning. If so, keep it warm.

7. If your frying pan is ovenproof, transfer it to the oven. Alternatively transfer the fish to a small baking tray and then into the oven. Cook for 5–7 minutes or until only just cooked through.

8. Just before serving the fish, rewarm the sauce then stir in the parsley, as leaving it in the hot sauce for too long will discolour it to khaki.

9. To serve, ladle a few spoonfuls of the parsley sauce onto 2 plates, place the fish on top and arrange the bacon over the fish.

Smoked trout fishcakes with walnut sauce

I love a fishcake, a stalwart piece of comfort food, but they are often too complicated, with too many ingredients. I believe a fishcake should be simply about fish and potato. The ratio of fish to potato here is perfect, thanks to some advice from Arnie, a kind cook with a café in Whitby who, despite his squashed nose and granite stature, has a sensitive touch in the kitchen. His is the best fishcake I have ever eaten!

Do use smoked haddock if you prefer. Being cold-smoked, the haddock will require pre-cooking. Arnie baked the haddock lightly rather than poaching it, as he bemoaned the pointless loss of flavour into the milk. I knocked up the sauce as an alternative to the inevitable tartare sauce. I hope you'll agree that it works very well.

Serves 2–4

› 300g King Edward potatoes, peeled and cut into pieces about the size of board-game dice
› 200g hot-smoked trout, any bones removed
› 3 tablespoons finely chopped fresh curly parsley
› 1/2 teaspoon flaked sea salt
› 2 tablespoons plain flour, sifted
› approx. 100g white breadcrumbs
› 2 free-range eggs
› 50g unsalted butter
› a splash of sunflower oil
› ground black pepper
› watercress, to serve

For the walnut sauce

› 2 tablespoons finely chopped walnuts
› 2 tablespoons mayonnaise
› 1 tablespoon crème fraîche
› grated zest of 1/2 small unwaxed lemon and a squeeze of juice, just enough to give the sauce an edge
› 2 good teaspoons grated horseradish (not sauce) from a jar, or 4 teaspoons from fresh root
› flaked sea salt
› ground black pepper

1. Put the potatoes into a pan and cover them with cold water. Bring them up to the boil, cooking them for 10–15 minutes, or until totally softened – a little overcooking is in fact good. Drain them and allow to stand until cool and dry.

2. While the potatoes cook, gently dry-fry the walnuts in a frying pan, swirling them continuously until they turn a shade or two darker and have a lovely toasted smell. Do not burn them. Allow them to cool.

3. Combine all the other ingredients for the sauce, stir in the walnuts, season, and then leave to one side.

4. Preheat the oven to 200°C/fan 180°C/gas 6.

5. Flake the trout into pieces and put them into a bowl, adding the chopped parsley and a good grind of black pepper. Add the potatoes, breaking them up as you do so. Combine well and season with salt.

6. Fashion the fishcakes inside a pastry-cutter mould of about 6 or 7cm diameter, or shape them with your hands. When forming the cakes you will need to press and compact them a little to prevent them falling apart.

7. Put the flour on one plate, the breadcrumbs on another, and beat the eggs in a bowl.

8. Flour both the flat sides of each fishcake – do not flour the circumference as they will be only shallow-fried. Now very carefully dip the floured sides in the beaten egg and then into the breadcrumbs, and repeat until all the cakes are done. If your cakes are collapsing, keep them in the mould until crumbed, as this helps keep everything together.

9. Put a small frying pan on the hob and heat the butter and oil. Put the fishcakes into the pan – they should sizzle immediately. However, do not cook them too fast and burn the breadcrumbs; just regulate the heat accordingly.

10. Cook the fishcakes on one side for 4 minutes or so, until a deep golden colour. Turn over and fry for 2 minutes more, then put the cakes into the oven for 6 minutes.

11. Serve with the walnut sauce and accompanied by watercress.

Red mullet with courgettes

Red mullet is a particular favourite fish of mine. It's two for one – a wonderfully full-bodied yet slightly flaky meat with the very noticeable taste of shrimps and small crabs, its favourite food. A mullet's love of feeding on such things also gives it its beautiful flamingo-pink colour. If very, very fresh, red mullet livers are delicious sautéed and should be eaten with oil, garlic, parsley, lemon and bread.

Courgettes are a wonderful companion for mullet, both colour-wise and in taste. These ingredients remind me of shopping in southern France under the dusty shade from plane trees. I choose my fish and vegetables in the warm market air, carrying the lingering smells of cafés, pastis and cigarettes. Wandering home to cook, I eat the ends of the baguettes along the way and the rest with this as lunch. We are always very quick to cut the stalk off the courgette, but when it is young it is as delicious as the flesh – you decide.

Serves 2

› 3 medium courgettes, sliced very thinly lengthways, stalks and all
› 1 tablespoon olive oil, plus extra for the dressing and oiling the fish
› 200g tinned borlotti beans, rinsed and drained
› a handful of fresh basil leaves
› 2 small cloves of new season's garlic or good dry garlic, hard and with no green shoots, sliced paper-thin
› a good squeeze of fresh lemon juice
› 1 teaspoon flaked sea salt, plus extra for seasoning the courgettes
› 2 medium red mullet, each approx. 350–400g, scaled, de-gilled and gutted
› 2 big sprigs of fresh rosemary, leaves picked off and very finely chopped

1. Preheat the grill to its hottest setting, with the oven shelf set as close to the element as possible.

2. Lay the courgettes on your largest baking tray and paint both sides with the oil. Place the courgettes under the grill and cook for 8–10 minutes, until they are charred and softened.

3. Remove the oven tray, turn the courgettes and return to the grill for a further 8–10 minutes, until nicely charred. (They should be limp and properly blackened in places on both sides, not half-heartedly browned, as they are tastier when beaten up by the grill.) Don't turn off the grill.

4. When they are cooked, transfer the courgettes to a bowl and add the beans and basil leaves. Mix in the garlic, lemon juice and a very generous glug of oil. Season to taste with sea salt, if need be.

5. Slash the fish, only very lightly, three times on each flank. Rub each one all over with olive oil and love. Mix the rosemary with the sea salt and season the fish, taking care to rub the seasoning into the slashes.

6. Place the seasoned fish under the grill – but not so close that they burn before the flesh is cooked. After 5 minutes, turn the fish over and do the other side – when done, they should be browned and quite crisp.

7. Serve the fish with the courgettes, beans and basil.

Fried herrings with curried potato salad

I cooked this in Stockholm, in a van famous for its herrings. Oddly enough, curry powder crops up quite a lot in the Swedish storecupboard, so I decided to incorporate it into a potato salad. The meal used to coat the herrings was very fine when compared to the oats I normally fry them in at home, so I have suggested Ready Brek for the oatmeal preparation instead.

You can make the mayonnaise by cheating with some shop-bought to which you then add an extra egg yolk, mustard and vinegar. However, it's very easy to make, so I suggest doing it from scratch as the result, in this case, will be better.

Serves 4

› 400g baby new potatoes, skins on
› 1 small red onion, finely diced
› 20g bunch of fresh dill, fronds roughly chopped
› 4 medium herrings, scaled and filleted
› 1 free-range egg, well beaten
› 40g plain Ready Brek, seasoned with 1 teaspoon flaked sea salt
› 50g unsalted butter
› a splash of sunflower oil

For the mayonnaise

› 2 free-range egg yolks
› 1 tablespoon German mustard or French's hot-dog mustard
› 2 good teaspoons medium curry powder
› $1^{1}/_{2}$ teaspoons caster sugar
› 20 ml (1 tablespoon plus 1 teaspoon) white wine vinegar
› 1 teaspoon flaked sea salt
› 150ml sunflower oil
› 50ml olive oil

1. Put the potatoes in a saucepan and just cover with water. Bring to the boil and cook for 15–18 minutes, until tender but not overcooked. Drain and allow to cool or, to cool them faster, aid them with a brief spell in cold water and drain again. When they have cooled, slice the potatoes into rounds $^{1}/_{2}$cm thick.

2. In the meantime, make the mayonnaise. Put the egg yolks into a mixing bowl and add the mustard, curry powder, sugar, vinegar and sea salt. Beat with an whisk or hand blender, very slowly drizzling in the oils until you have a lovely thick mayonnaise. If the mayo is too thick, while still in the process of making it, loosen it with a splash of warm water. It should be only just stiff, but not runny or droppy. If, for some odd reason, it splits, add another egg yolk and a tad more mustard to a new bowl, then drizzle the disaster back into the new base, where it will hopefully behave. Follow with a little more oil to balance the extra egg.

3. Mix the onion, dill and cooled potatoes into the curried mayonnaise and check the seasoning.

4. Pat the herring fillets dry with some kitchen paper or a cloth, then sandwich the fillets together in pairs, with the skins on the outside.

5. Dip the double fillets into the beaten egg, then roll them in the oats.

6. Melt the butter in a large frying pan but do not allow it to burn (adding some sunflower oil will help with this). Gently fry the fillets over a low–medium heat for approximately $2^{1}/_{2}$ minutes on each side, or until crisp and golden.

7. Divide the potato salad between 4 plates and serve the herrings on top.

Smoked mackerel spread with pickled cucumber

It's not potted, it's not pâté, so spread was my last option, as whip didn't sound great. Hot buttered toast, white wine and lounging kitchen chat are great accompaniments for my smoked mackerel spread.

Serves 6–8

› 4 smoked mackerel fillets (not the peppered ones in this case, although they would work), skin removed
› 100g fridge-cold unsalted butter, cut into cubes
› 2 heaped teaspoons Dijon mustard
› 1½ heaped teaspoons good horseradish sauce (optional)
› 4 tablespoons crème fraîche
› a good squeeze of fresh lemon juice
› 3 spring onions, finely sliced at an angle
› ground black pepper
› hot buttered toast, to serve

For the pickled cucumber
› 1 medium cucumber, peeled, halved lengthways, deseeded with a teaspoon and cut into 5mm slices
› 1½ teaspoons flaked sea salt
› 100ml white wine vinegar
› 20g white sugar
› 1 Earl Grey tea bag

1. To make the pickled cucumber, mix the cucumber slices with the sea salt and leave to drain in a colander for 30 minutes, tumbling regularly.

2. In the meantime, in a small saucepan over a gentle heat, warm the vinegar with the sugar and, when the sugar has dissolved, drop in the tea bag. Leave it there for only 20 seconds or so, as you want to taste it but not too much. Do not press the teabag against the side of the pan before removing it. Leave to cool.

3. Add the cucumber to the vinegar and stir through well. It is good whether it is left for a while or only briefly soaked.

4. Break up 3 of the mackerel fillets and drop them into a food processor. Add the butter, mustard, a good grind of black pepper and the horseradish sauce, if using. Blend until very smooth.

5. Turn out into a bowl and stir in the crème fraîche. Season with lemon juice, just enough to give the mackerel an edge but not to dominate it.

6. Break up the remaining mackerel fillet and gently stir it through the spread. This will give it a roughness – a dimension it needs.

7. Transfer the mackerel spread to a serving bowl and scatter over the spring onions. Serve with the pickled cucumber and a fork to pick it out of the vinegar. Eat with hot buttered toast.

'Hot buttered toast, white wine and lounging kitchen chat are great accompaniments.'

Things with bread

4B bread

In Yorkshire when filming I chanced across this delicious bread over breakfast. But why the name? Well, I was staying in a *B&B* and this *bread* was *black* – 4Bs! The thing was that, had this been entered into any of the county shows at which we had been filming, I am sure it would have scooped prizes. Ann, who runs the immaculately clean Waterford House along with her husband Martin, very sweetly gave me the recipe after I finished practically the whole loaf with her very nice raspberry jam. It's got a definite element of pumpernickel about it, but it's more giving, with a wonderful pliancy and tenderness. Its genius is that it requires no kneading. I generally do not eat it for breakfast but couple it with pickled herrings and cured salmon. Although most of the recipes in this book do not take so much time to prepare, this is about as utterly easy as bread gets, so I decided it would cross the finish line.

This is very good with smoked and cured fishes, or with cheese and jam on top together, in that Scandi way. I am writing the measurements for the ingredients exactly as they were scribbled down for me – the recipe joyously straddles both imperial and metric systems.

Makes 1 loaf

› butter
› oats
› 8oz wholemeal flour
› 8oz plain flour
› 1 tablespoon caraway seeds
› 1/2 teaspoon salt
› 1 × 7g sachet of dried yeast
› 125ml black treacle
› 325ml warm water

1. Butter the inside of a loaf tin lightly. Throw in a handful of oats and shake them tactically around the inside so that the oats stick to the butter and coat the interior.

2. In a large mixing bowl combine the flours, seeds, salt and dried yeast.

3. Ooze the black treacle into a measuring jug and add the warm water. Stir both together until the treacle has dissolved. Stir into the flour mixture until well combined.

4. Scrape the bread mixture into the waiting loaf tin and leave to rise in a warm place with some clingfilm very loosely covering the tin (remove the clingfilm before the bread sticks to it). Leave for an hour or so or until doubled in size.

5. Preheat the oven to 200°C/ fan 180°C/gas 6.

6. Just before the bread goes in the oven, put an oven tray on the bottom shelf and pour in about 5mm of boiling water. Scatter a few more oats over the top of the loaf then put it into the oven and cook for 50 minutes.

7. When the bread is ready the water should have boiled away, allowing the loaf to develop a crispy crust. The loaf should be quite dark, so don't think it's burnt. Turn it out of the baking tin and give it a final 5 minutes in the oven without it. Allow to cool before serving.

Squash with borlotti beans on bread

Like the Courgette and Barley on page 143, this is a recipe that brings an almost palpable calm to my table and mind because of its pleasing simplicity. Of course I like a variety of cuisines and dishes that may demand different levels of difficulty, but when I eat things like this, I just feel such an uncomplicated satisfaction. I ate a variation of this in a small trattoria in Tuscany – the bread is my substitution for barley. The menu was short and delivered verbally, while outside banks of mist and rain rolled over the grey valley. The light from the doorway of this establishment, when we left, was similar in warmth and inviting colour to the squash I had eaten. It was a good dinner, as I was also falling in love with my wife.

'When I eat things like this, I just feel such an uncomplicated satisfaction.'

Serves 4

› 50g unsalted butter
› 1 small onion, finely diced
› a good pinch of dried rosemary
› a good scratch of nutmeg
› 650g squash (try an interesting variety such as Red Onion, Blue Hubbard or butternut), seeds removed, flesh peeled and coarsely grated
› 200g tinned borlotti beans, drained and rinsed
› 4 slices of good rustic sourdough, bread, foccacia or ciabatta
› a very generous slug of your best olive oil, plus extra for brushing
› 1 clove of garlic, halved lengthways
› flaked sea salt
› ground black pepper
› aged pecorino or Parmesan cheese, to serve

1. Melt the butter in a large pan over a medium heat. Add the onion, rosemary and nutmeg and gently sauté for 10 minutes or so, until the onion is very tender.

2. Throw in the squash and stir it into the onion. Gentle cooking sounds should be heard, but nothing too fierce. Put the lid on the pan and cook for an hour or so, stirring now and then. If the mixture catches on the bottom of the pan a little, this is fine – but not so much that the mixture burns. Loosen with a dribble of water if need be.

3. Preheat the grill to high.

4. When it is ready, the rich squash purée should be seasoned generously with sea salt and pepper. Stir in the beans, then put the pot back on a low heat and bring back to a simmer.

5. Paint the bread with a little olive oil and grill it on both sides, then rub with the garlic.

6. Stir the olive oil into the squash and beans.

7. Put the toasts on 4 plates, spoon over some of the squash, then grate or shave the cheese over the top.

Broad beans for bread

This recipe was originally called broad bean hummus but I find it irksome to mislabel things. It's not really hummus but rather hummus-inspired, as it has no chickpeas in it, or tahini, for that matter. I hate the word 'dip', and broad bean purée sounds like something that should be accompanied by a gammon chop, whereas this is a nibble.

The bigger broad beans by the end of the season are far from tender and are really fit only for stewing or mashing. Prepared like this they are delicious and a wonderful colour to boot.

The walnut oil makes an intriguing alternative to purely olive oil, but leave it out if nuts result in hospital.

Serves 2–4 with a pre-dinner drink

› 1kg large broad beans in their pods (to give 250g when podded)
› 1 small clove of good hard garlic (no green centre or shoot), finely sliced
› 2 tablespoons olive oil
› 2 tablespoons walnut oil
› juice of 1/2 small lemon, just enough to give the beans an edge
› flaked sea salt
› fresh mint, to garnish
› focaccia or pitta bread, toasted if you wish, to serve

1. Bring a pan of water to the boil and meanwhile pod the broad beans with the radio on.

2. Boil the beans for 5–6 minutes, or until totally soft. Drain them, then immediately plunge them into iced water until cold – to retain their colour. Drain again.

3. Peel the skins off all the beans and put them into a bowl.

4. With a stick blender, blitz up the beans with the garlic, slowly adding the oils. Add the lemon juice, followed by a dribble of cold water if the mixture needs loosening. It should only just hold its shape and should be smooth and creamy. Add sea salt to taste, bearing in mind that it needs a little more than you might think.

5. Garnish with fresh mint and serve with focaccia or pitta bread.

'Prepared like this, end-of-season broad beans are delicious and a wonderful colour to boot.'

Mushrooms on toast a different way

I normally cook mushrooms on toast very simply – butter, lemon juice, parsley and garlic. This version, however, is inspired by the way that mushroom sauce tends to be made in Scandinavia, although normally morels are used there instead of dried porcini.

Serves 2

› 30g dried porcini mushrooms
› 150ml boiling water
› 40g unsalted butter, plus extra for buttering the toast
› 1/2 medium onion, very, very finely chopped
› 1 1/2 tablespoons plain flour
› 50ml double cream
› 50ml full-fat milk
› 50g Lancashire cheese, grated
› a scratch of nutmeg
› 1/2 teaspoon flaked sea salt
› 2 good slices of bread, from a white bloomer
› a slice of good-quality ham (optional)
› ground black pepper

1. Tip the mushrooms into a small bowl, cover with the boiling water and leave for 15 minutes.

2. Meanwhile, melt the butter in a small frying pan and sauté the onion for approximately 8 minutes, or until totally tender: no less will do. Do not colour the onion. Stir in the flour and cook gently for 30 seconds to 1 minute, stirring all the time, then put the pan to one side.

3. Remove the mushrooms from the water, squeezing any excess liquid back into the bowl (do not discard the liquid). Put the mushrooms on a chopping board and chop roughly but fairly small.

4. Put the onion roux back on the heat and, when it starts foaming again, start adding the mushroom water. A sauce will start to form – stir it constantly to eradicate any lumps. You want a consistency that you really wouldn't call a sauce but something that more resembles a stiffish béchamel. Stir in the chopped mushrooms.

5. Now add the cream and milk. Add the cheese and let it melt into the sauce. Bubble it back to something a bit stiffer than 'saucy'. Add the nutmeg, sea salt and a good grind of black pepper. Take the pan off the heat and allow the sauce to cool a little.

6. Toast the bread, then butter it on one side and lay it on a baking tray.

7. Preheat the grill to medium. Spread the cooled mushroom sauce thickly over the toast. If you want to, lay a slice of ham on top of the toast before adding the mushroom sauce.

8. Put the toasts under the grill and toast until hot and well browned.

9. Accompany with a cup of tea and hopefully some David Attenborough on the telly. Mind you, it makes a good breakfast as well.

Mum's TV pilchards on toast

We used to eat this a lot. Always served up cut into small squares on kitchen paper and eaten in front of those not-forgotten classics such as *Dad's Army*, *Fawlty Towers*, *The Muppet Show*, *Knight Rider*, *The Man from Atlantis*, *Fantasy Island* and *The A-Team*. Mum would have chopped and changed the ingredients according to what was in the storecupboard, but I am using the ones that turned up most of the time.

Serves 4 as a quick snack

> 15g unsalted butter, plus extra for spreading
> 1 small onion, finely chopped
> a good pinch of dried thyme
> 1 tablespoon tomato purée
> 3 good tablespoons tomato ketchup
> a dash of Tabasco , to taste
> a good splash of Worcestershire sauce or soy sauce
> a few green olives, chopped
> 1 heaped teaspoon drained capers
> 2 × 100g cans of pilchards in extra virgin olive oil, drained
> 10g fresh parsley, leaves finely chopped
> a small squeeze of fresh lemon juice
> 4 slices of cheap pre-sliced brown bread
> ground black pepper

1. Melt the butter in a small pan and cook the onion with the thyme until totally soft.

2. Add the tomato purée and ketchup, followed by the Tabasco and Worcestershire or soy sauce.

3. Drop in the olives and capers and add an industrial bombardment of black pepper.

4. Add the pilchards and mash everything together with a fork. Stir in the parsley and finally add the lemon juice.

5. Preheat the grill, toast the bread and spread liberally with butter. Divide the mixture between the toast slices and pop them under the grill until sizzling. Cut in halves or quarters and serve on kitchen paper in front of the television.

Weekend breakfast anchovy and Parmesan baked eggs

Although these are simple to make and the results fairly speedy, this luxurious little egg dish seems better suited to a more leisurely breakfast, maybe enjoyed at 11am in pyjamas or a dressing gown with combed hair and crisp newspapers. Toast is a happy playmate, but so is a piece of haddock that can be painted in butter and baked in the oven at the same time as the eggs, although this will extend the cooking time by a few minutes.

You will need 6 × 9-cm diameter ramekins.

Serves 6

› 6 little knobs of unsalted butter, plus extra for greasing
› 12 teaspoons finely grated Parmesan cheese
› 300ml single cream
› 8 free-range eggs, plus 2 egg yolks
› 6 salted anchovies in olive oil, drained
› 1 small clove of good garlic, finely chopped then smushed with the side of a knife
› 1 generous teaspoon Dijon mustard
› 1/2 teaspoon cayenne pepper
› ground black pepper
› 6 slices of buttered toast, for soldiers, to serve

1. Preheat the oven to 200°C/fan 180°C/gas 6.

2. Thoroughly grease the inside of each ramekin with a little butter, then use half the Parmesan to dust the insides of the buttered ramekins.

3. Place the cream, 2 eggs and 2 yolks, anchovies, garlic, mustard, cayenne pepper and the remaining Parmesan in a measuring jug and blitz it using a stick blender.

4. Crack 1 egg into each ramekin, taking care not to break the yolk.

5. Top up each ramekin with the cream–custard mixture so that it comes up over the top of the egg yolk.

6. Pop a knob of butter on top of each ramekin and season with a grind of black pepper.

7. Place the ramekins in a baking tray and carefully pour 1cm of just-boiled water into the baking tray between them.

8. Put the tray of ramekins in the oven and bake for 13–15 minutes or until the custards retain only the slightest jiggle when the baking tray is gently knocked. The yolks should be runny but the whites cooked.

9. Serve the custards warm, with hot buttered toast soldiers.

'...this luxurious little egg dish seems better suited to a more leisurely breakfast.'

Sardines with sweet-and-sour onions on sourdough

Originally I developed this recipe as a pizza for Pizza Express, but it did not make it to the *pizzaiolo*'s marble slab. It was truly delicious, but decidedly a little too left-field for their market. I moved it on to bread and it has become one of my favourite staples at home. If you are making a pizza dough, please try it like this too.

What did the Dalai Lama say to the *pizzaiolo*? Make me one with Everything.

Serves 2

› 3¹/₂ tablespoons extra virgin olive oil
› 2 medium onions, halved and very finely sliced
› 1 bay leaf
› 1 tablespoon fresh thyme leaves
› a pinch of dried chilli flakes
› 2 cloves of garlic, very thinly sliced
› 2 tablespoons white wine vinegar
› 2 tablespoons sultanas, rehydrated with a little hot water
› 2¹/₂ teaspoons caster sugar
› ¹/₂ teaspoon flaked sea salt, plus extra for seasoning
› 2 large slices of sourdough bread
› 2 medium sardines, scaled, filleted and patted dry
› 5g Parmesan cheese, finely grated
› 1 tablespoon fresh lemon juice
› a scratch of zest from an unwaxed lemon
› fresh marjoram or mint
› 1 tablespoon toasted pine nuts
› ground black pepper

1. Heat 2¹/₂ tablespoons of the oil in a frying pan large enough to fit the onions comfortably. Drop in the onions with the bay leaf, thyme leaves and chilli and sauté very gently, stirring often – they must not colour at all. Cook for around 15 minutes, or until the onions are totally soft.

2. Drop in the garlic and cook for a further 2 minutes. Do not let the garlic burn.

3. Only when the onions are very tender and nothing less, add the vinegar and sultanas and keep cooking until the liquid has evaporated.

4. Stir in the sugar and cook until it has dissolved but not caramelized. Season with the sea salt and transfer to a bowl.

5. Preheat the grill to high and toast the slices of bread.

6. Divide the onion mixture between the slices of toast, brushing any leftover oil in the bowl over the sardines. Lay the sardine fillets on top of the onion mixture, skin-side up. Drip a little more oil over them, and then scatter over the Parmesan.

7. Place the toasts under a hot grill, not too close to the element, and grill for 4¹/₂–5 minutes, or until the sardines are brown.

8. Meanwhile, mix the remaining oil with the lemon juice.

9. Remove the sardines from the grill. Grind some black pepper and a little sea salt over the top of each fillet, then add the lemon zest and drizzle with the oil and lemon dressing.

10. To serve, scatter over a good amount of chopped marjoram or mint (marjoram is that much better) and the toasted pine nuts.

Potted shrimps, Margot's way

I quite like the top layer of butter here that texturally resembles broken old shoe polish rattling around a tin, but by blending a lot of shrimp with the butter Margot Henderson's recipe makes for something much better than the traditional version. So here is Margot's method. It's brilliant.

Serves 8

- › 300g salted butter
- › 3 × 90g packets cooked and peeled brown shrimps
- › a very generous scratching of nutmeg (half a nut)
- › 1 tablespoon finely chopped fresh dill (optional, according to your mood)
- › ground black pepper
- › flaked sea salt

To serve
- › toast or melba toast
- › lemon wedges

1. Clarify the butter by melting it in a saucepan over a low heat. Small white islands of milk solids will float to the top. Skim them off. White sediment will also fall to the bottom, so carefully pour off the clear golden butter when ready. This process will take about 10 minutes. Set aside about 50g of the clarified butter and reserve it for the top of the shrimps.

2. Put the rest of the butter into a bowl or food-processor bowl with two-thirds of the shrimps. Add the nutmeg, but err on the side of caution, as you can put it in but you can't take it out. Add a good grind of fine black pepper, but don't add any salt yet, as the shrimps and salted butter may do the job well without additional seasoning.

3. With a stick blender, or in the food processor, blitz together the shrimps and the butter. Turn out the mixture and then stir in the remaining one-third of the shrimps.

4. Taste once more and season with sea salt and extra pepper if need be. Bear in mind that the taste of the nutmeg should definitely be prevalent but not overpowering. Stir in the dill, if using. Put the prepared shrimps into a jar or bowl, pour over the reserved butter and leave in the fridge for a couple of hours to firm up.

5. Before serving, let the shrimps stand for a little while out of the fridge so that they are not too cold and stiff. Serve with plenty of toast or melba toast, and wedges of lemon. Potted shrimps should also consider themselves doing well if they find themselves pushed into the cleft of a steaming hot and crispy jacket potato.

Mussels and leeks on toast

This is a favourite, so easy and utterly pleasing. Toast is a vehicle for so much more than we give it credit for. Long live life on toast!

Serves 2–4

› 500g large live mussels in the shell, cleaned and de-bearded
› 200ml white wine or cider
› 40g unsalted butter, plus extra for spreading on the toast
› 400g leeks (around 4 medium leeks), sliced 5mm thick
› a couple of scratches of nutmeg
› 1 large clove of garlic, crushed
› 4 slices of good white sourdough bread
› a squeeze of fresh lemon juice
› 2 tablespoons fairly finely chopped fresh flat-leaf parsley (optional)
› flaked sea salt
› ground black pepper
› lemon wedges, to serve

1. Check the mussels and discard any that are open and that don't close when you tap them. Put a saucepan large enough to contain the mussels over heat and drop in the mussels, followed by the wine or cider. Once the liquid is bubbling, steam the mussels for 2–3 minutes, stirring once halfway through the cooking time. You want to take them off the heat when they have only just opened and are slightly underdone. This is because they will be briefly cooked again.

2. Drain the mussels in a colander over a bowl and leave them to cool (discard any that have not opened). Put the delicious juices to one side. Into the same pan in which you cooked the mussels, drop a large knob of butter and melt it.

3. Drop in the leeks, scratch over the nutmeg and sauté slowly for about 10 minutes or so, stirring occasionally, until the leeks are beautifully soft and tender. Don't rush. There should be no watery element to them at all. While the leeks are cooking, take the mussels out of their shells and put them into a small bowl.

4. Stir the garlic into the leeks and cook for 2 minutes more, then add the mussel juices and simmer rapidly for around 5 minutes until the liquid has almost totally evaporated. There should be a luxurious creamy quality to the leeks and nothing you would describe as watery.

5. Load the slices of sourdough bread into the toaster.

6. Stir the mussels into the leeks. Season with lemon juice, the parsley (if using), sea salt and plenty of black pepper. Don't be tempted to cook the mussels for too long, as they will become overcooked – 30 seconds will suffice.

7. Butter the toast and put the mussels and leeks on top (add an extra knob of butter at this point, if you like). Serve with lemon wedges and eat immediately.

Skagen

As a fan of devouring motorway service-station prawn mayonnaise sandwiches when driving up and down the UK, I was delighted to discover this popular Swedish classic, which is a much more luxurious and interesting delight than the aforementioned garage fare. In short, I became addicted to it when filming in Scandinavia. Although it is normally just a prawn affair, I did have it with crab mixed in as well, and it was particularly good. I recommend the 4B Bread you will find on page 104 as a good coupling with this recipe.

Serves 4–6

> 4 heaped tablespoons mayonnaise, chilled
> 4 heaped tablespoons full-fat crème fraîche, chilled
> 450g cooked plump peeled Atlantic prawns (not king or tiger prawns)
> 1/2 small red onion, very finely diced
> 30g fresh dill fronds, roughly chopped, plus a few delicate stems to garnish
> a good squeeze of fresh lemon juice, to taste
> toast, either a good sourdough or my 4B Bread (*see* page 104)
> 50g jar of salmon caviar (optional)
> flaked sea salt
> ground black pepper
> lemon wedges, to serve

1. Combine the mayonnaise and crème fraîche in a bowl.

2. Remove the prawns from the packet and very gently squeeze them, just enough to get rid of any excess water (there may be none), as this can make the sauce too runny. Do not squeeze them like a flannel. Add the prawns to the bowl.

3. Add the onion and dill and stir everything together gently. Squeeze in just enough lemon juice to give the sauce a noticeable edge but not to overpower it. Add any additional sea salt you feel is needed, and a grind of black pepper.

4. Drop the toast into the toaster and, when it is done, cut each slice in half widthways. Spoon a very generous amount of skagen on top.

5. Add a fat dollop of salmon caviar, if using, on top and decorate with dill stems.

6. Serve with wedges of lemon.

Grilled venison sandwich

The roe deer really is prince of the forest. Tread very quietly through the sticks and leaf litter and you will find them staring, as they most likely saw you first. Within a blink or random thought they dissolve as if by magic... in fact, sometimes I think it is. With their cloven feet, careful posture, penetrating look, and small pronged candle-drip antlers, these creatures hold a very special place in my heart. I will eat them, as we have many, but am as happy to see them trotting between the hazels and oaks. Cooking the meat and toasting the bread over charcoal does make a superior sandwich, although cooked conventionally it's very good too! Venison does not respond well to being well done, as it is very lean.

Serves 4

› 600g roe or fallow deer strip loin
› olive oil, for rubbing
› 1 teaspoon dried thyme
› flaked sea salt
› ground black pepper

For the green sauce
› 2 tablespoons finely chopped fresh tarragon
› 2 tablespoons finely chopped fresh marjoram
› 1/2 tablespoon baby capers
› 1/2 medium shallot, finely chopped
› finely grated zest and juice of 1/2 unwaxed lemon
› 4 tablespoons olive oil
› 1 small clove of garlic, finely chopped

To serve
› 8 slices of sourdough bread, medium sliced
› 1/2 teaspoon Dijon mustard per sandwich

1. Combine all the ingredients for the green sauce. Season to taste and leave to one side until needed.

2. Rub the meat all over with olive oil and season with the thyme, sea salt and black pepper. On a griddle or a barbecue, sear the loin for approximately 4–6 minutes on each side, or until you think it's right. It should be well coloured on the outside and pink within. Allow to rest for 8 minutes or so. This is important as, during this time, the meat will finish its cooking and become relaxed and tender.

3. Toast the bread (preferably on a barbecue) and spread half the slices with the mustard.

4. Slice the venison and lay it on top.

5. Apply lots of green sauce and the remaining toasted slices and eat the sandwiches immediately.

'The roe deer is prince of the forest. These creatures hold a very special place in my heart.'

Chard, bacon and walnuts on toast

This combination was born of an odd day filming when I had pulled a muntjac deer out of someone's car radiator, in a hotel car park at night, after his vehicle had appeared to swallow it like a pike. The shocked man did not want it, so in the interests of a free meal we took it. We went on to film next to the most bountiful tree I have ever seen and left with a bin liner of wet walnuts. Later we brought a box of fine-looking chard after we had stopped to pick some roadside porcini. We ate the deer with the mushroom sauce, while the milky walnuts were cooked up with the chard. What a great dinner. The winner for me was the chard and walnuts – the director's idea, I might add.

I have adapted the recipe using the more matured walnuts you will find in the shops and have added bacon. It has also evolved on to toast and become a favourite of my home repertoire. Try to find shelled walnuts with a nice pale skin, as they are less bitter. Crack them yourself if you know they are good 'uns.

Serves 2

> 3 large chard leaves, rinsed and cut into 1cm slices
> 25g unsalted butter, plus extra for buttering the toast
> 100g smoked bacon lardons
> 1/2 medium onion, finely sliced
> 50g walnuts, roughly broken
> a good scratch of nutmeg
> 2 large slices of sourdough bread, or other bread of your choice
> a good squeeze of fresh lemon juice
> flaked sea salt
> ground black pepper

1. Bring a saucepan of water to the boil for the chard and blanch it for 6 minutes or so. Drain and refresh under cold water, then drain again very thoroughly.

2. Meanwhile, melt the butter in a frying pan and sauté the lardons for 5 minutes. Add the onion and walnuts and continue to cook for a further 7 minutes, stirring often, until the onion is completely soft and golden, translucent and unarguably tender. Grate in the nutmeg followed by a heavy grind of black pepper.

3. Put your chosen bread into the toaster and plunge it. Add the chard to the frying pan and turn it through the contents. Season with the lemon juice and sea salt if need be.

4. Butter the toast, then turn the chard mixture out on to it and enjoy with a cup of tea or a bottle of cider.

Vegetables

Quick beans 'n' greens

This is a quick and tasty dish to cobble together and a good advertisement for not needing a hunk of meat or fish to feel satisfied. Chipotle is one of several things I refer to as a magic ingredient. It is, arguably, good with almost everything. A bowl of this is what I call a 'power-up'.

Serves 2

› 40g lard
› 1 large onion, medium diced
› 2 chipotle chillies, or 3 if very small, seeds and stalks removed, rehydrated in warm water, then drained and very finely diced
› 1/2 teaspoon dried oregano
› 3 large cloves of garlic, very thinly sliced
› 1/2 Knorr or other squidgy chicken stock cube
› 400g can of pinto or black beans, half the juice drained away
› 1/2 teaspoon flaked sea salt (optional), plus extra for the greens
› 250g kale or spinach
› a little olive oil (optional)
› a squeeze of lime juice (optional)
› ground black pepper

1. Melt the lard in a saucepan over a medium–low heat and sauté the onion with the chipotle chillies and oregano until the onion is totally softened, golden and only just beginning to catch.

2. Throw in the garlic and cook for a further 2 minutes or so, stirring a lot so that the onions do not colour any more.

3. Add the stock cube and plenty of black pepper, then tip in the beans. Stir it all together and bring to a simmer, then cook until the beans are hot. If they appear to thicken too much, loosen them with a little water until they are the consistency of Heinz baked beans. Check the seasoning again and add the sea salt if you think it's needed.

4. If using kale, bring a saucepan of water to the boil and dunk it in. Cook until tender but not too soft, then drain. If using spinach, collapse it in a hot frying pan with the oil and drain well. Season with sea salt and pepper.

5. Dish up both beans 'n' greens on a plate and add a little squeeze of lime if you so wish.

'A bowl of this is what I call a "power-up".'

Courgette fritti with ricotta

Jumbled on to a plate, crispy and hot with a wedge of lemon sitting next to them, this is courgettes at their best. Arguably anything deep-fried is enjoyable, but I really think they come into their own here. It struck me as a good idea to replace the veal chop with which I would normally accompany these courgettes with something else for a change.

Serves 4–6

› 250g ricotta cheese, drained
› 10g each fresh marjoram, mint and basil, leaves very finely chopped
› 3 unwaxed lemons
› 4 medium courgettes
› 1 tablespoon flaked sea salt, plus extra for seasoning
› sunflower oil, for deep-frying
› 130g strong white flour
› 1/2 teaspoon bicarbonate of soda
› 200ml chilled fizzy water
› good olive oil
› ground black pepper

1. Mix the ricotta with the herbs and the grated zest of 1 of the lemons. Season with a good pinch of sea salt and some pepper. Chill until you are ready to serve the courgettes.

2. Chop the courgettes into batons roughly 8cm long. Place them in a colander, sprinkle with 1 tablespoon sea salt and lightly toss them about. Place the colander over a bowl and leave to drain for 30 minutes.

3. Heat the oil to 170°C in a deep-fryer or medium saucepan. (Take care never to leave hot oil unattended.)

4. Sift just 80g of the flour and the bicarbonate of soda into a large bowl and add a small pinch of sea salt. Add the fizzy water very gradually, whisking carefully to remove any lumps but taking care to avoid beating out all the bubbles.

5. Tip the remaining 50g of flour into a bowl.

6. When the courgettes have had their draining time, in batches of around 8–10 batons, first dip the courgettes into the flour, dusting off any excess, then dip them into the batter using tongs. Briefly allow the excess batter to drip from the courgettes before you carefully drop them into the hot oil.

7. Fry each batch of courgettes for around 1 minute, or until the batter is crisp and a light golden colour.

8. Transfer the cooked courgettes to a baking tray lined with kitchen paper to drain while you continue with the next batch.

9. Serve with the chilled ricotta, splashed with a little olive oil and with the rest of the lemons cut into wedges to squeeze over.

'Jumbled on to a plate, crispy and hot, this is courgettes at their best.'

Beetroot salad with blackcurrants

This vital little salad came about purely through wonky logic. The main ingredients are the same kind of colour, they both have a sweetness, blackcurrants have a tartness the beetroot needs, they grow next to each other in my garden. There's nothing more pleasing than a successful hunch. The dressing calls for an ingredient I have been less than kind about – balsamic vinegar. I feel it is carelessly splashed about on everything in an unwelcome tide that floods the deli counters and kitchens of Britain. Here it behaves well.

If boiling beetroots from fresh, please cook them with the skin, whisker and trimmed stem left on as, if cooked peeled, they will lose both colour and flavour.

Serves 2

› 12 fresh baby beetroots of mixed colours, root whiskers and stalk tufts left on, halved
› a little rapeseed oil
› 250g fresh blackcurrants
› 1/2 teaspoon caster sugar
› 1 teaspoon balsamic vinegar
› 1 teaspoon wholegrain mustard
› 2 tablespoons olive oil
› 10 fresh chives, very finely chopped
› 1 tablespoon very finely chopped fresh curly parsley

1. Preheat the oven to 170°C/ fan 150°C/gas 3½.

2. Toss the beetroots in the rapeseed oil and roast them in the oven for 45 minutes–1 hour, or until tender.

3. In the meantime, in a pan over gentle heat, collapse 200g of the blackcurrants with a little sugar, the vinegar and 3 tablespoons cold water for around 5 minutes, until totally softened. Pass through a sieve, pushing with the back of a ladle to extract as much of the purée as possible. Allow to cool. It should not be watery but should rather be a smooth, loose-ish purée.

4. When the beetroots are done, allow them to cool for 10 minutes, until just warm, and peel. Toss them in a salad bowl with the mustard and olive oil.

5. Drizzle over the blackcurrant purée and scatter a few of the remaining whole blackcurrants here and there. Sprinkle over the herbs.

6. This is delicious eaten with duck or more simply with a very fresh, rindless, tangy soft sheep's cheese.

Bloody beetroot

Ben, a clever young cook, prepared this as part of a shooting lunch for a rag-tag band of hungover duck-shooting chefs. I thought it was delicious. I have duplicated his presentation as well.

Serves 4

› 4 medium fresh beetroots, root whiskers and stalk tufts left on
› 200ml tomato juice
› scant ¹/₂ teaspoon celery salt
› 2 teaspoons Henderson's relish or Worcestershire sauce
› a good splash of sherry vinegar
› a small squeeze of fresh lemon juice
› a few drops of Tabasco (optional)
› a few sprigs of watercress
› a little olive oil, for dressing
› flaked sea salt
› ground black pepper

1. Cook the beetroots in boiling salted water for about 40 minutes, or until tender. Allow them to cool, then remove the stalks and skins whilst taking great care not to snap off the long root whiskers.

2. While the beetroots are cooking, mix the tomato juice, celery salt, Henderson's relish or Worcestershire sauce, sherry vinegar, lemon juice and Tabasco into a bowl. Season with ground black pepper.

3. Thickly slice each beetroot into 4 across its girth. Spoon some of the dressing in a neat puddle in the middle of each plate. Place the beetroots, as if intact and root whisker facing the sky, on to the sauce, then slightly offset each piece once the beet is in place.

4. Garnish with watercress, dressed with the oil and sea salt.

Caponata

The southern Italian dish caponata has many variations, as one would expect from a region where almost every family is blessed with good cooks. Delicious eaten outside on a hot day and pushed on to some bread with a fork, it is also a wonderful accompaniment to lamb, goat, chicken or fish cooked over charcoal. I would note here that it is just as good when served at room temperature as it is hot.

Generally in the UK the aubergine is a misunderstood vegetable, all too often found undercooked and lurking in a depressing-looking ratatouille or watery vegetable lasagne. The secret is to get them well greased with oil (but not sodden) and then hit them hard with heat. Whether you are charring or roasting aubergines, a good colouring seems really to bring out their taste. The aubergines are cooked only when a knife pushed into them slides through with no resistance. Anything less and they are simply not ready, toothsome in a nasty way and often causing tickly irritation to the roof of the mouth. Treated right, they are a favourite.

It might not surprise you to know that aubergines belong to the nightshade family, closely related to tomatoes, peppers, chillies and potatoes.

Serves 4

› 3–4 tablespoons olive oil
› 1 medium red onion, finely diced
› 2 medium aubergines, cut into cubes twice the size of sugar lumps
› 1¹/₂ tablespoons baby capers taken from vinegar, or the equivalent amount of sliced caper berries
› 2 tablespoons red wine vinegar
› 1 teaspoon dried oregano
› 4 cloves of good garlic, finely sliced
› finely grated zest and juice of ¹/₂ small unwaxed lemon
› 8 canned anchovies in olive oil, drained
› 2 tablespoons tomato purée
› 1 teaspoon caster sugar
› flaked sea salt
› ground black pepper
› fresh parsley and mint, to garnish

1. Heat 2 tablespoons of the oil in a saucepan and cook the onion over a medium heat for 10–12 minutes, or until totally softened. Remove from the pan with a slotted spoon, pressing as much of the oil as possible back into the pan. Put the onion on a plate and set aside. Add the rest of the oil to the pan and cook the aubergines over a medium heat until they have picked up some good colour and are completely soft.

2. Put the onion back into the pan, along with the capers, then add the vinegar and let it evaporate. Now add the oregano, followed by the garlic, lemon zest and anchovy fillets, and cook, stirring often, until the anchovies have totally disintegrated.

3. Add the tomato purée and the sugar, and cook for a further minute or so. Loosen everything just a little with cold water so that the mixture appears moist rather than wet, then season with sea salt and black pepper.

4. Either allow to cool to room temperature or serve hot, scattered all about with a mixture of fresh parsley and mint.

Cauliflower and cannellini bean soup

There is something very gentle and soothing about a white soup. Its warm paleness and delicate but tasty flavour are most calming. This is a soup for the turn of the weather, sunlit orange and bronze cold autumn days.

Serves 4

> › 1 cauliflower (approx. 500g)
> › 25g unsalted butter
> › 750ml good tasty chicken stock
> › 1 sprig of fresh rosemary
> › 1 tablespoon flaked sea salt, plus extra for seasoning
> › 410g can of cannellini beans, rinsed and drained
> › 4 tablespoons double cream
> › a little milk (optional)
> › grated Parmesan cheese, for sprinkling
> › olive oil, for drizzling
> › ground black pepper

1. Cut the cauliflower into small florets – you should end up with around 450g after trimming. Put into a clean saucepan with the butter and cook it gently for about 5 minutes. Pour over the chicken stock. Cover the pan and bring to a simmer, then cook for around 12–15 minutes, or until very tender – don't be tempted to add extra water or the finished soup will be too thin.

2. Remove the leaves from the rosemary sprig and put in a pile on a board with the sea salt. Chop the rosemary and sea salt together until very fine – a coarse chopping will not do. Set aside.

3. Add half the beans to the soup and blitz with a stick blender until smooth. Stir in the rest of the beans and the double cream. Loosen with a little milk if it's too thick. Warm through gently, then season to taste with a touch of sea salt and some black pepper – show modesty with the salt, as more will be added when scattered about with the rosemary.

4. Ladle into warmed soup bowls. Sprinkle with the rosemary salt mix, a grind of pepper and a good grating of Parmesan, and scribble over with a little olive oil to finish.

'This is a soup for the turn of the weather, sunlit orange and bronze cold autumn days.'

Special Sunday carrots

My wife always chops the carrots into little discs, which galls me – I have no desire to be time-warped back to school with visions of giant aluminium pans full of sloppy mince and carrots, the smell combining with steam drifting off mountains of overcooked rice under heat lamps. Raised voices, pushing, jostling, Formica trays, scratched Pyrex, dirty cutlery, clatter-clatter... All can be revived with a glassy stare through an overcooked carrot. I like my carrots simply peeled and, if very large, quartered or halved lengthways or at least cut into sizeable batons.

This luxurious little finish really is the business, and is fabulous with pink slices of lamb chump or chops. Needless to say, the large-carrot approach really aggravates my wife, who says they look lazy and carry a bogus simplicity. I love her punchiness.

Serves 4–6

› 6 good medium carrots, peeled, with a small quiff of trimmed green stem attached, and split in half lengthways
› 2 medium banana (long) shallots, halved lengthways, then thinly sliced
› 25g fridge-cold unsalted butter, plus a further 50g, cut into cubes
› 2 tablespoons red wine vinegar
› 2 teaspoons soft light brown sugar
› 2 tablespoons chopped fresh curly parsley
› flaked sea salt
› ground black pepper

1. Boil the carrots in a saucepan of salted water for 8–10 minutes, or until certainly tender while retaining some firmness. Try to synchronize the carrots with the rest of the meal.

2. Meanwhile, in another pan, big enough for the carrots, sauté the shallots gently in 25g of the butter for 8 minutes or so. When they are done, tip in the vinegar and add a healthy grind of black pepper. Boil until half the vinegar is left, then add the sugar.

3. Beat in the cubes of butter 2 at a time with a wooden spoon until the shallots are emulsified, thickened and creamy.

4. Stir in the carrots and parsley and add a small splash of hot water if the shallots look a little un-saucy.

Artichokes with shallot, dill and carrots

I ate this in France for lunch with my mother. The restaurant was empty and huge and overlooked a very wide, muddy river with a sluggish flow, its banks dotted with enormous willows that trailed their branches in the current. I cannot, however, remember for the life of me where it was. We ate by a window that magnified the hot sun and got very drunk on cold Chablis. This is a good lunch eaten simply with bread or some thin ham.

Serves 2

> 2 large globe artichokes, stems removed
> 4 really good, tasty medium carrots, the kind you might find in a bunch, peeled and with a 5mm tuft of green stem left on
> 1/2 medium banana (long) shallot, halved and thinly sliced
> 1 large fresh bay leaf
> juice of 1/2 lemon
> 1/2 tablespoon extra virgin olive oil per plate, plus extra for the artichokes
> 1 1/2 teaspoons Dijon mustard
> 1 1/2 tablespoons white wine vinegar
> 1 teaspoon caster sugar
> a small pinch of flaked sea salt
> 1/2 tablespoon capers
> 1/2 tablespoon chopped fresh dill
> 5g fresh tarragon leaves

1. Sit the artichokes on their bases in a large saucepan on the hob and cover with water. Bring to the boil, then cover with a lid and cook for 30–40 minutes, until tender but not over-soft. When the artichokes are ready, drain and refresh in cold water, then drain again.

2. While the artichokes are cooking, place the carrots and bay leaf in a smaller saucepan and cover with cold water. Bring the water to the boil and cook for 10–12 minutes, or until they are very tender. Drain the carrots and refresh in cold water, then drain again. Remove the bay leaf. Slice the carrots into thirds on a steep diagonal.

3. Peel off all the petals from the artichoke, leaving you with the heart. Remove the furry choke completely, using a teaspoon, then cut each heart into 4 lengths. Put the artichoke pieces into a bowl and toss immediately with the lemon juice and a little olive oil. Not only will this season them nicely, but it will also stop them oxidizing and turning blue.

4. In a small bowl, combine the Dijon mustard with the white wine vinegar and sugar and season with a small pinch of sea salt.

5. Add the carrots, shallot, capers, dill and tarragon to the bowl of artichokes and toss with the vinaigrette.

6. Divide the salad between 2 plates and drizzle with oil to serve.

Tacos de rajas

In my view the only treatment for a poblano chilli is to char it, as it then becomes one of the most sensational tastes I know. With an intense blue-green flesh, it has a buttery taste that sometimes comes with a tolerable heat. Allowed to ripen to red, it becomes fiercer, and in Mexico it is usually dried at this point, becoming chilli 'ancho'.

In its green form the poblano chilli is really worth trying to get your hands on. You can order them from Joy Michaud at Peppers by Post (www.peppersbypost.biz).*

Alternatively try to grow some – you can get the seeds from the same address. Because poblanos are not the easiest things to source, I have also suggested green peppers. Try to find some really dark green specimens, as they retain a better colour once charred.

You can buy proper corn tortillas from the Cool Chile Company (www.coolchile.co.uk). Soft corn tortillas can be bought in supermarkets but are very inferior.

Serves 4

› 4 poblano chillies or green peppers
› 2 tablespoons vegetable oil
› 2 medium onions, sliced
› 1 teaspoon dried oregano
› 1 teaspoon ground cumin
› 1 potato, cut into 1cm cubes
› 150g tub of crème fraîche or soured cream
› 1/2 teaspoon sunflower oil
› 8 small corn tortillas
› 50g Wensleydale cheese, grated
› 1 small bunch of fresh coriander, roughly chopped
› 1/2 large lime, cut into small segments
› flaked sea salt
› ground black pepper

1. Turn on a gas hob, if you have one, and lay the poblanos or peppers over the naked flame. Turn them regularly until they are totally black, blistered and charred. When you think they are done, may I suggest that they probably are not? They want to be as black as night all over. This will take about 7–9 minutes. Alternatively put them under the grill, very close to the element, and turn them as they blacken. Allow to cool.

2. Place a deep-sided frying pan over a medium heat, add the vegetable oil and fry the onions for 8–10 minutes, or until deep brown and tender. Do not burn them. Add the oregano, cumin and potato, combine everything well, then briefly fry, tossing often, for 1 minute or so.

3. Add 200ml water to the pan and simmer the onions and potato for 10–12 minutes, by which time the water should have evaporated, leaving the potato tender. The water must be properly cooked away, but add a splash more if the potato is underdone.

4. Meanwhile rub the charred skin of the poblanos or peppers away from the flesh with your thumb or a little kitchen paper. Don't be tempted to remove the skin with the aid of a tap or you will lose the wonderful burnt taste. A few black flecks left here or there don't matter. Open them up, discarding the stalks and seeds, then rip them lengthways into ribbons about 1cm wide.

5. Just 1 minute before the potato is done, stir in the pepper strips and season, then add the crème fraîche or soured cream and turn off the heat. Check the seasoning again.

6. Gently heat a large frying pan and add the tiniest dash of sunflower oil. Heat the tortillas for about 1 minute on each side, until very floppy. Sometimes a little flick of water from the ends of your fingers helps get them loosened. Serve them hot, with a generous spoonful of creamy pepper mix on top. Scatter over the cheese and coriander, then add a little squeeze of lime juice. Enjoy immediately, with very cold lager.

Marinated mushrooms

This is a very fresh and delicious way to enjoy mushrooms. I would suggest not using any black-gilled varieties, such as Portobello, as they stain the liquor an inky colour. This dish can be very pretty when made with wild mushrooms, like the yellow chanterelle, blewit, amethyst deceiver and young cep (penny bun). But just making it with chestnut, closed cap, enoki or oyster mushrooms produces a delicious salad too.

Serves 4

› 300g mushrooms (choose from chestnut, closed cap, enoki, oyster, yellow chanterelle, blewit, young cep or amethyst deceiver)
› juice of 1 small lemon
› 2 small cloves of good hard garlic, sliced paper thin
› 4 tablespoons extra virgin olive oil
› 1 teaspoon flaked sea salt
› 1 tablespoon fresh tarragon or chervil leaves
› 1¹/₂ tablespoons fresh chives, finely chopped
› ground black pepper
› toasted sourdough or rustic bread, to serve

1. If the mushrooms are tight and firm, slice them lengthways at a width of about 3mm. If they are very small or thin-stemmed, add them whole; if they are funnel-shaped, then tear them. Put them into a bowl, squeeze over the lemon juice, and add the garlic, oil, sea salt and a good grind of black pepper.

2. Leave the mushrooms to marinate for about 20–30 minutes, gently turning once during this time, then stir the herbs into the mushrooms.

3. Eat with some thinly sliced sourdough or rustic bread, grilled, griddled or toasted over charcoal.

'This dish can be very pretty when made with wild mushrooms.'

Baked shallots in cream

I'm sure I've said it many times, but shallots, like all onions, are the unsung heroes of the kitchen. Here's a recipe where they shine in their own right, a kind of meaty but vegetarian dish, so to speak, to accompany a good hunk of brilliant sourdough. Note that, although the cream may look curdled, it is not – it will be silky smooth as hoped.

Serves 2, or 4 as an accompaniment to beef or lamb

> 8 medium banana (long) shallots, topped and barely trimmed at the root end, then peeled
> 25g unsalted butter
> 2 tablespoons red wine vinegar
> 1 teaspoon soft light brown sugar
> 1/2 teaspoon flaked sea salt
> 1/2 teaspoon dried rosemary
> 100ml double cream
> 10g Parmesan cheese, finely grated
> ground black pepper
> good sourdough bread, to serve

1. Cook the shallots in a saucepan of boiling water for 12–15 minutes, or until soft, then drain.

2. Preheat the grill to high, making sure the shelf is approximately 12cm away from the element.

3. Melt the butter in a snug little ovenproof frying pan, add the shallots and sauté them gently for 8 minutes or so, turning once. When they are ready, they should be a rich brown on both sides. Don't rush this stage and burn the butter.

4. Pour over the vinegar and simmer for 30 seconds. Scatter over the sugar and turn the shallots over once more. Allow the sugar to caramelize on to the shallots for around 3–4 minutes, turning them a couple of times. Scatter with the sea salt and dried rosemary.

5. Remove the frying pan from the heat, pour off some of the excess butter, and then pour the cream over the shallots.

6. Sprinkle the Parmesan and a good grating of black pepper over the top and put the shallots under the grill for 4–5 minutes, or until well browned and just bubbling.

7. Serve with a good sourdough.

'Shallots, like all onions, are the unsung heroes of the kitchen. Here's a recipe where they shine in their own right.'

Fattoush salad

When I think of fattoush salad, it's always because I'm suddenly craving it, in a climbing-the-walls kind of way. Once eating it, I can't stop – it's so refreshing, pleasing and clean – and although it's very enjoyable without any accompaniment, I usually serve it alongside some simply chargrilled lamb chops or chicken livers. The right amount of salt is vital to this salad being a success or disappointment, so add a little more than you normally would.

Sumac, used a lot in Middle Eastern cookery, is a berry that is dried and ground. Although still not widely available in supermarkets in the UK, it is relatively easy to find in Middle Eastern supermarkets and some corner shops. Sumac gives a sour twang similar to hibiscus and, ultimately, lemon. Make the salad with lemon juice if need be, whilst remembering that sumac has its own particular taste and adds prettiness to the salad, being a deep red-purple in colour.

Traditionally this salad would be made with stale rather than fresh pitta bread. Use whatever you have, although there is more gratification in saving things from the bin. Make this salad and serve it straight away. Like proud sheikhs, once dressed, fattoush does not respond well to being made to wait.

Serves 4

› 2 pitta breads, stale or fresh, halved lengthways, then cut into 2cm ribbons widthways
› 4 tablespoons olive oil
› 2 big grabbing handfuls of pea tops, or 2 baby gem lettuces, shredded
› 2 good ripe medium tomatoes, roughly chopped, or 16 good cherry tomatoes, halved
› 6 radishes, very thinly sliced
› 2 medium carrots, very finely sliced or cut into matchsticks
› 1/2 medium red onion, halved again, then very finely sliced
› 1/2 large cucumber, peeled and diced a little smaller than sugar lumps
› 10 leaves of fresh mint, stacked and cut into ribbons
› 1 small bunch of fresh dill, fronds picked from stalks (optional)
› 1 large handful of fresh parsley leaves
› juice of 1/2–3/4 lemon
› flaked sea salt
› a very small pinch of chilli powder
› a good sprinkle of sumac

1. In a small frying pan, gently sauté the pitta pieces in 1 tablespoon of the oil over a medium heat for around 4–5 minutes, turning once, until crisp and golden. Drain on kitchen paper and leave to cool.

2. In a bowl combine all the salad, vegetables and herbs. Add the cooled pitta pieces.

3. Dress with the lemon juice, the remaining oil, some sea salt and chilli, then sprinkle with the sumac.

4. Serve immediately, alone or with some chargrilled lamb seasoned with a little cumin and sea salt.

Sweet potatoes with coriander butter and lime

This is not a recipe – in fact it's the kind of thing that, if I found it in another cookbook, would probably give me a very physical feeling of being swizzled. But!... I must put it in, as it is totally delicious.

Make sure you wash the sweet potato skins – they are good and should be eaten.

Serves 2

› 2 large sweet potatoes
› a generous pinch of flaked sea salt
› 1¹/₂ tablespoons finely chopped fresh coriander
› 80g unsalted butter
› lime wedges, for squeezing

1. Preheat the oven to 210°C/ fan 190°C/gas 6¹/₂.

2. Wash the sweet potatoes in cold water and place them on a baking tray. While still wet, sprinkle them with the sea salt.

3. Put the sweet potatoes into the oven and bake for 1 hour, or until totally squishy, with signs of dark sugars seeping from the skin.

4. Mash the chopped coriander into the butter.

5. To serve, split the potatoes, drop half the butter into each one, pinch over the sea salt and squeeze in some lime juice.

Courgette and barley

First put on the table by my wife, a very good cook who surprisingly does not enjoy cooking, this is now a Warner favourite for autumn weather, very simple food that delivers such joy, not only in taste but also in its frugality. The secret is not to rush the cooking.

On pearl barley: few things in life really annoy me, but of those things that do, food terminology really does. 'Deconstructed' – WHY? (Unless you simply don't know how to assemble something.) 'Pan-fried' would be most customers' educated guess, unless the chef also uses tennis rackets. Pearl barley risotto is one such thing that, although it is no crime, blurs the understanding of what a dish should be – like cassoulets containing chorizo and bouillabaisses containing salmon. *Riso*, in Italian, means rice, *not* pearl barley. So I can't help it, but 'pearl barley risotto' annoys me. When complaining it is always good to offer an alternative, but, alas, I have nothing to offer in this instance except moaning.

Serves 2

> 50g pearl barley
> 1 medium onion, finely diced
> 70g unsalted butter
> a good scratch of nutmeg
> 500g good firm courgettes, roughly chopped quite small
> Lancashire or Wigmore cheese, for melting (optional)
> flaked sea salt
> ground black pepper

1. Tip the pearl barley into a small saucepan, cover with water and bring to the boil. Cook for approximately 40–45 minutes, or until plump and giving but still with a firmness. Drain in a colander.

2. While the pearl barley cooks, gently sauté the onion in the butter with a good scratch of nutmeg for about 15 minutes. Throw in the courgette flesh and allow to sauté slowly with the lid on for 1 hour, stirring every now and then. If it catches just a little, that's fine, but the catching should be stirred out and, in the end, the courgettes should have cooked down to a really tasty, rich and concentrated purée.

3. When the courgettes are ready they will start to just catch the bottom of the pan all the time. Stir a few times, then stir in the pearl barley and bring it up to the temperature of the courgettes.

4. Season with plenty of sea salt to bring out the subtle courgette flavour, and a grind of black pepper.

5. Should you happen to have it, a rindless squidge of Lancashire or Wigmore cheese is good melted into your humble courgette and barley.

6. Serve accompanied with a glass of cold cider.

Boston beans, Dad's way

This really reminds me of my dad and how much I miss him. He'd make this for his boys and it always seemed to be when we could sit down and watch *The Dukes of Hazzard*.

Serves 2–4

› 60g unsalted butter
› 1 large onion, medium diced
› 1 teaspoon dried thyme, plus a little extra for the breadcrumbs
› 1 bay leaf
› ¼ teaspoon ground cloves (optional)
› 1 tablespoon tomato purée
› 2 × 400g cans of baked beans
› 1 heaped tablespoon black treacle
› 8 rashers of smoked streaky bacon, sliced to postage stamp size
› 4 medium vine tomatoes, sliced to about 5mm thickness
› 2 large handfuls of breadcrumbs
› 1 teaspoon ground black pepper
› 1 large clove of garlic, very finely chopped, then smushed with a little salt
› flaked sea salt
› buttered curly kale, to serve (optional)

1. Preheat the oven to 200°C/fan 180°C/gas 6.

2. Melt half the butter in a frying pan and sweat the onion with the thyme, bay leaf and ground cloves (if using). Cook for approximately 10 minutes, stirring often, until the onion is golden and totally softened but not coloured or browned.

3. Add the tomato purée and cook for a minute or two, stirring constantly. If it catches a little, this is good. Add the beans followed by the black treacle, and stir until everything is thoroughly combined.

4. In a separate small frying pan, fry the bacon pieces until nicely coloured and crisp, then remove, leaving the fat in the pan.

5. Take a medium ovenproof dish and put half the bean mixture into the bottom. Scatter over half the crispy bacon, then add the remaining beans, followed by the rest of the bacon. Season the tomatoes with a little sea salt, place them on top, dot with half the remaining butter, then put the dish into the oven and cook for 20 minutes, or until bubbling, with the tomatoes beginning to crisp at the edges.

6. Meanwhile, put the breadcrumbs into the frying pan that the bacon was cooked in and add the rest of the butter, the black pepper and a little more thyme. Stir constantly over a medium heat until the breadcrumbs are golden, and just before they get to this stage, stir in the garlic, making sure it's distributed through the breadcrumbs, not in one lump.

7. Take the beans out of the oven and cover them with the breadcrumbs, then put them back into the oven for a further 5 minutes.

8. Serve immediately, maybe accompanied by buttered curly kale.

Unctuous slow-roasted tomatoes

This is a wonderful way to deal with a glut of tomatoes, and the result is utterly delicious. They crop up through the book in a couple of other recipes (Roast Chicken, Tomato and Celeriac Remoulade Sandwich on page 120, and Tomato and Goats' Cheese Salad on page 186). The residual tomato oil from the jars is fabulous in dressings and for storing olives in. Excellent in sandwiches, the tomatoes are also delicious eaten with anchovies and capers, or accompanying pretty much any meat or fish.

The point of the ingredients is to ramp up the sweet and the sharp and to exaggerate the essence of the tomato. The recipe is very quick to assemble. Then, once the tomatoes are in the oven, you can just go off and do something else, although I would advise taking the kitchen timer with you.

Makes 2 small jars

› 10 medium vine tomatoes, cut in half downwards from stalk to base
› 1/2 teaspoon soft brown sugar for each half tomato
› 2 tablespoons red wine vinegar
› a pinch of dried chilli flakes for each half tomato
› a small knob of unsalted butter for each half tomato
› olive oil
› a few sprigs of fresh thyme
› flaked sea salt
› ground black pepper

1. Preheat the oven to 140°C/fan 120°C/gas 1 and line a large baking tray with baking parchment.

2. Arrange the tomatoes, cut-side up, in rows on the tray. Scatter the brown sugar on top of each tomato half, then the vinegar, the chilli and a generous pinch of sea salt and pepper. Dot each tomato with butter and a little olive oil and scatter over the thyme sprigs.

3. Put the tomatoes in the oven and leave them there for about 4–5 hours. They should be a little browned around the edges. The flesh should be withered yet moist, but with no obvious wateriness.

4. When they are ready, turn the tomatoes over so they lie face down in the rich sweet syrup that will have seeped out of them on to the baking tray. Allow them to cool. Once they have cooled, turn them the right way up again and make sure that any sticky juices are scraped back over them.

5. Either use the tomatoes straight away or put them into small jars, cover them with olive oil and use them over the following 2 weeks.

'A wonderful way to deal with a glut of tomatoes, and the result is utterly delicious.'

Tomato and basil tarts

Years ago, when I was a moody teenager rather than a sulky adult, my mum used to take me to a snazzy restaurant called the Caprice. I always ordered the same things, the tuna with lentils and the tomato tart. I have since become friends with Mark Hix, who used to be the head chef there, and he has generously given me this recipe so that you may enjoy it.

Serves 2

> plain flour, for dusting
> 250g block of puff pastry
> 3 large ripe tomatoes (about 350g)
> 3 heaped tablespoons sun-dried tomato pesto
> 3 tablespoons olive oil, plus 1 teaspoon for brushing
> 6 large fresh basil leaves
> 1 good clove of new season's garlic, or other good garlic (no green shoots), very finely chopped
> just over 1/2 tablespoon fresh lemon juice and a scratch of lemon zest
> flaked sea salt
> ground black pepper

1. Preheat the oven to 220°C/fan 200°C/gas 7 and line a baking tray with baking parchment.

2. Scatter some flour over a clean work surface and roll out the puff pastry to about the thickness of a £1 coin. Take a side plate roughly 19cm in diameter and lay it upturned on the pastry. Pull a knife all the way around the outside. Repeat. Separate out the discs from the spare pastry and transfer them to the lined baking tray. Reserve leftovers for whatever you please.

3. Pop the baking tray into the oven and cook the tarts until you estimate them to be half risen. At this point quickly slice the tomatoes.

4. Remove the pastry discs from the oven and press them down with a spatula.

5. Turn the oven temperature up to 240°C/fan 220°C/gas 9.

6. Spread the pesto over the pastry discs in an even layer, leaving a border of roughly 1.5cm of un-pestoed pastry all the way around.

7. Lightly pat the slices of tomato with kitchen paper to absorb some of the moisture. Working from the centre of each pastry disc, quickly lay the tomatoes on the pastry, overlapping in concentric circles, until totally covering the pesto area – you will need around 15 slices per pastry disc.

8. Brush the tomatoes with 1 teaspoon of the olive oil. Do not season. Put the tarts back into the oven for a further 8 minutes.

9. In the meantime, stack the basil leaves and slice them finely. Put them into a small bowl with the 3 tablespoons of olive oil, the garlic, lemon juice and zest.

10. Remove the tarts from the oven. The tomatoes should be wrinkly at the edges and not be remotely watery. The uncovered rim of pastry should be golden brown.

11. Season with plenty of sea salt and pepper and fleck all over with the basil dressing. Serve immediately.

Cooling cucumber and fennel with yoghurt

A friend and I went to visit his aunt one exhaustingly hot day in the Massif Central, in France. Climbing out of a sticky car, we'd arrived on a building site and hobbled over rubble covered in snakes of pipe. The sound of cicadas was deafening and the heat haze shimmered with unwavering intensity; the sun demanded you bow your head while the white dusty ground demanded you squint. There was nowhere to look and my legs were burning.

Lying next to a crusted cement mixer by an alluring swimming pool was a most extraordinary woman. She was about sixty, brown as tanned hide – and as leathery too – spread-eagled on a lounger with a pastis in one hand and half a substantial cigar alight in the other. Her face was cracked with a thousand wrinkles and her hair was a shock of tight white curls. In addition to an ill-fitting electric-blue bikini, she wore cut-off rubber boots and had a strong masculine assurance about her. I'd immediately decided I liked her before she rose up and greeted us with real warmth in deep gravelly French. She ushered us into the shade of her house where, around her table, I discovered she was a fabulous and delicate cook. We dined on simple but exquisite roasted chicken cooked with garlic, rosemary and peppers, alongside fried potatoes. However, it was this recipe that I really found to be interesting, simple and soothing. It was served chilled and accompanied by very good fresh *flute*, the kind of French stick that, thankfully, is becoming easier to find in the UK.

Serves 6

> 1 large cucumber, peeled, halved lengthways, seeds scooped out, very thinly sliced
> 1 heaped teaspoon flaked sea salt, plus extra for seasoning
> 1 teaspoon fennel seeds
> 1 medium bulb of fennel, base trimmed, stalks removed and fronds retained if any, then halved and very thinly sliced across
> 2 medium banana (long) shallots
> 5 tablespoons olive oil
> 3 tablespoons dry white wine, such as Chablis or Sancerre, from a fresh bottle
> 1 1/2 tablespoons white wine vinegar
> 2 large cloves of good garlic (no green shoots), very, very finely chopped
> 400ml fresh full-fat plain yoghurt
> grated zest and juice of 1/2 unwaxed lemon
> 1 tablespoon finely chopped fresh mint
> 2 tablespoons finely chopped fresh tarragon leaves
> 2 tablespoons finely chopped fresh dill
> ground black pepper
> French stick or sourdough, to serve

1. Throw the cucumber into a colander and add the sea salt. Mix together well and leave to drip over the sink for 30 minutes.

2. Bring a small saucepan of water to the boil with the fennel seeds in it. Drop the fennel into the water and simmer until only just beginning to be tender while retaining a crunch. Drain and set aside to cool.

3. Very gently sauté the shallots in a frying pan in half the oil – they must not be browned at all – and, when they are tender, add the fennel. Pour in the wine and vinegar, then evaporate it until almost gone. Allow to cool.

4. Squeeze the cucumber of as much remaining water as possible, holding it as you would if you were squeezing a wet flannel. Put it into a bowl with the shallots, fennel and garlic.

5. Flop the yoghurt on top, followed by the remaining oil, and combine gently. The consistency should be only a little thicker than that of pouring double cream.

6. Add the lemon zest and then squeeze in the juice. Now stir in all the herbs and adjust the seasoning with any further sea salt and a good grind of black pepper. Leave to chill in the fridge for at least 30 minutes. It should be very cool rather than cold.

7. Serve with French stick or a good crusty sourdough bread.

Asparagus, anchovy sauce and egg

Annually I moan that I have not eaten enough asparagus. Since 2012 I have made up for pretty much every year I consciously felt I missed out on. In fact I got rather bored with the inevitable hollandaise, melted butter or vinaigrette options and was looking for new ways of serving asparagus, the point of seasonal cooking, I might add. This is a very respectable summer lunch for when the weather is hot and you don't want to sit down to anything too substantial.

Serves 6

› 1 clove of good garlic (no green shoots)
› 1 tiny sprig of fresh rosemary
› 3 free-range eggs, plus 1 egg yolk
› 70g white anchovies (vinegared in oil, not the brown salted ones)
› 50ml full-fat milk
› 60ml olive oil
› a splash of double cream (optional)
› 30 stalks of British asparagus, trimmed
› flaked sea salt
› ground black pepper

1. Finely chop the garlic and rosemary and put into a small bowl with the egg yolk and anchovies.

2. Warm the milk in a small pan, taking it off the heat just before it simmers. Pour it over the anchovy mixture and blitz it with a stick blender. Pour in the olive oil very slowly until you have a nice creamy dressing. This sauce can be finished with a little double cream, if you like.

3. Place the eggs in a pan of cold water and bring to the boil, then boil for 4 1/2 minutes. Drain the eggs and cool them quickly in cold water.

4. In a separate saucepan, put the asparagus into enough boiling water to cover it. Bring back to the boil and cook until just tender. Drain, then run the asparagus under cold water and dry thoroughly.

5. Arrange 5 stems of asparagus side by side on each plate. Swiftly cut the eggs in half so as not to let the middle run out, and place one half on each plate of asparagus. Season the eggs with sea salt and pepper and drizzle over some of the dressing.

Asparagus cigars

This is a great little snack for parties, so simple, a winning time-saver. Double or triple the recipe, as the cigars disappear quickly. I took the inspiration from the amazing cook Jeremy Lee, who normally makes this with salsify.

Makes 16

› 16 stalks of British asparagus
› 4 sheets of ready-made filo pastry
› 50g unsalted butter, melted
› 2 handfuls of finely grated Parmesan cheese
› flaked sea salt
› ground black pepper

1. Preheat the oven to 210°C/fan 190°C/gas 6½.

2. In a saucepan, cook the asparagus in enough well-salted boiling water to cover it, cooking it for only 1 minute once the water has come back to the boil. Drain, cool in cold water, then drain again, making sure it's thoroughly patted dry with a tea towel.

3. Cut the asparagus stalks two-thirds of the way down, saving the lower stems for a chilled soup.

4. Brush the pastry lightly but thoroughly all over with melted butter. Cut each sheet into 4. Place an asparagus spear along the bottom of each filo piece and roll up snugly but not over-tightly. It should have about 2 rolls – any more and the layers of filo get too built up, resulting in a crispy outside but a disappointing centre.

5. Picking each cigar up with your fingers, brush the outside with butter again, then scatter the grated Parmesan thoroughly over the top.

6. Lay the cigars on a tray lined with greaseproof paper, with the outside edge of the filo underneath (this stops them unravelling when they cook). Grind over a heavy bombardment of black pepper.

7. Cook the cigars in the oven for about 10–15 minutes, or until deep golden and very crisp.

8. Pile up on a plate and serve.

'A great little snack for parties, so simple, a winning time-saver.'

Fennel gratin

Fennel is a particular favourite of mine. I love it raw in salads, or shaved into hot water with a few of its seeds as a tea. Roasted, it's a brilliant accompaniment for pork – in fact, for any meat – and is delicious puréed with fish. All in all I eat a lot of it, and here's a great treatment for it that I like to eat without any meat or fish.

Serves 2 as a light lunch

›   2 large bulbs of fennel, split in half lengthways through the thinner side
›   75g unsalted butter
›   5 cloves of garlic, cut into thin slivers
›   40g fresh white breadcrumbs
›   a handful of chopped fresh parsley, tarragon or basil
›   40g Parmesan cheese, finely grated
›   2 teaspoons fennel seeds, gently toasted in a dry pan
›   finely grated zest and juice of 1 unwaxed lemon
›   a pinch of dried chilli flakes
›   flaked sea salt

1. Bring a saucepan of water to the boil and drop in the fennel. Cook for 15 minutes or so, until tender. Drain, in a colander, then pat dry with kitchen paper and set aside.

2. Melt the butter in a medium ovenproof frying pan. Add the garlic and very gently fry it until golden, stirring occasionally. Do not burn it! Remove the garlic from the pan with a slotted spoon.

3. Turn up the heat a little and add the fennel, flat-side down. The halves should not overlap. Fry, taking care not to burn the butter, until the fennel flesh is deep golden in colour (about 20 minutes). Leave it alone and don't be tempted to fiddle.

4. In a bowl mix the breadcrumbs with the herbs, Parmesan, fennel seeds, lemon zest and juice and chilli flakes. Tip in about a tablespoon of the butter from the fennel pan and stir it through thoroughly.

5. Turn the fennel over so that the coloured side is facing up, then season with sea salt and scatter with the fried garlic. Scatter the breadcrumb mixture over the top and place under a hot grill, not too close to the element, until nicely golden brown.

6. Eat accompanied by a good cold glass of Sancerre or Macon.

Quick soupe au pistou

I first ate this soup as a boy with my parents and their friends in a restaurant in the south of France. It arrived in a huge bowl, with the pistou spooned all over the top. There was enough for three servings each. Typical of any meal involving Warners, the serving bowl was emptied. Then came another huge copper pan of quails cooked with cognac and garlic. I remember the whole meal and, bizarrely, have a vivid picture in my mind of the state of my napkin at the end of it.

Normally this is a soup that takes time, what with soaking the beans and then cooking them. However, with a storecupboard that forever boasts a selection of canned flageolet, cannellini or borlotti beans, this version is a quickie for those with less time or an impatient hunger. You can use one kind of bean or a variety. Make this at any time of the year, but it is really good when tomatoes are at their best.

Serves 6-8

> 3 tablespoons olive oil
> 1 medium onion, finely chopped
> 1 medium leek, halved and sliced into 1cm rounds
> 4 medium carrots, medium diced
> 200g green beans, topped (not tailed) and chopped small
> 2 fat cloves of really good garlic (no green shoots), finely sliced
> 2 bay leaves
> 1/2 teaspoon dried thyme
> 1/2 teaspoon dried rosemary
> 3 courgettes, medium diced
> 100g frozen peas
> 2 ripe beef tomatoes, skinned and coarsely chopped
> 400g waxy potatoes, peeled and medium cubed
> 1.2 litres water
> 2 good fistfuls of chard, chopped into ribbons, stalk and all
> 3 teaspoons flaked sea salt
> 2 × 400g cans of beans, such as white or green flageolet, borlotti or haricot, rinsed and drained
> ground black pepper
> a good loaf of sourdough, to serve

For the pistou

> 3 fat cloves of really good garlic (no green shoots)
> 1 1/2 teaspoons flaked sea salt
> 20 large leaves of fresh basil
> 2 ripe beef tomatoes, skinned and coarsely chopped
> 6 tablespoons olive oil
> 1 1/2 tablespoons fresh lemon juice

1. In a large saucepan or flameproof casserole, heat the oil and add the onion, leek, carrots, green beans, garlic, bay leaves and dried herbs. Cook gently until softened, about 10–12 minutes, then add the courgettes and cook for a further 5 minutes, stirring often. Add a big bombardment from the pepper mill.

2. Add the peas and tomatoes and cook for a further 5 minutes, stirring occasionally to prevent any catching, then add the potatoes followed by the water.

3. Bring to a simmer, cover lightly and cook for 15 minutes, or until the potatoes are ever-so-slightly overdone. Add the chard while the potatoes still have 5 minutes left to go. Season well with the sea salt – it seems like a lot but it's essential to bring out the flavour of the soup.

4. Stir in the beans. Bring the mixture to a simmer and turn off the heat.

5. While the soup sits, make the pistou. Chop the garlic and smush it with half of the sea salt with the side of the knife. Chop the basil roughly but fairly finely, using a sharp knife so as not to bruise it.

6. Mix the tomatoes, garlic, basil and oil in a bowl, and season with the lemon juice and remaining sea salt.

7. Serve the soup with the pistou and a good loaf of sourdough, warmed in the oven.

French bean and herb salad

Again and again I will say it – STOP topping and tailing your French beans! Certainly the stem end needs to come off, but the nose (which I presume is the tail) is only bean, after all, and looks better left on than cut off. Its removal is pointless and wasteful.

All herbs of the delicate variety can go into this salad, be they dill, basil, marjoram, mint, chervil, chives, parsley, tarragon, lovage or coriander (although I tend not to use the latter). Don't go overboard if you use lovage, as it's very powerful. Tougher herbs, such as rosemary, thyme, oregano and sage, have no place here and should volunteer for appropriate work elsewhere. Use the herbs you have, even if at a minimum. Don't drive to the shops unless planning to get other things for the week.

Generally I find French beans are undercooked, but treat them as you see fit (although they should be bitey rather than crunchy and never squeaky to the teeth!). This is a favourite salad of mine. Brilliant with all fish and meat.

Serves 2

› 250g French beans
› 50g fresh parsley, chives, mint, tarragon and lovage
› 1 medium banana (long) shallot or ½ small onion, halved lengthways and very finely sliced
› 1 clove of very good hard garlic, extremely finely chopped, then smushed with the side of a knife
› 2 good teaspoons Dijon mustard
› 1 tablespoon red wine vinegar
› 1 teaspoon caster sugar
› 3 tablespoons olive oil
› flaked sea salt
› ground black pepper

1. Cook the beans in boiling water until cooked (5 minutes is good), then drain. Cool under or in very cold water to refresh them, drain once more, then dry them. Put them into a salad bowl and toss with a little salt.

2. Pick the herb leaves from their stalks and simply cut the chives in half – they look better like this rather than being pointlessly chopped into mosquitos' bracelets. Add them to the bowl with the shallot or onion.

3. Combine the garlic, mustard, vinegar and sugar in a small bowl and gradually whisk in the oil until creamy. Season carefully and drizzle all over the salad.

4. Mix delicately and briefly and eat at once, as the salad will look bedraggled if prepared too far in advance.

Nasu dengaku (Japanese miso-glazed grilled aubergines)

I always order this in a Japanese restaurant if it's on offer. The recipe is truly superb, a good thing to do to an aubergine and a real umami blast-off. It's a fine ambassador for the banquet of vegetarian deliciousness that can be found across the globe. It's just the British concept of vegetarianism that is often so depressing. Lost for a simple lunch idea? Ditch the pasta salad and head for this!

'Lost for a simple lunch idea? Ditch the pasta salad and head for this!'

Serves 1–2

› 1 small (by which I do not mean baby) aubergine, stalk left on
› sesame oil, for brushing
› 50ml mirin
› 2 tablespoons soft brown sugar or dark runny honey
› 2 tablespoons red miso paste
› 15g piece of fresh ginger
› 2 teaspoons shoyu soy sauce
› 2 teaspoons toasted sesame seeds
› 1 large spring onion, finely sliced

1. Preheat the grill to high.

2. Cut the aubergine in half lengthways through the flesh and stalk. Cut a criss-cross diamond pattern fairly deeply across the flat face of the aubergine flesh. (Take care not to cut into the purple skin, however, otherwise your aubergine will lose its shape.)

3. Brush each aubergine half on the front and back with sesame oil and place under the grill. Cook, turning once, for about 15–20 minutes, or until totally tender and browned. Check while cooking to make sure that the aubergine is not so close to the element that it burns, but is not too far away to cook either.

4. While the aubergine cooks, pour the mirin into a small saucepan, bring it up to a rapid simmer and cook for $1^{1}/_{2}$ minutes. Stir in the sugar or honey, and the miso paste, then peel and grate the ginger and squeeze the juice into the pan but don't add the pulp. Cook the sauce over a very low heat for 30 seconds or so, then stir in the soy sauce.

5. Divide the sauce between the 2 aubergine halves, spreading it over the flesh, then put the aubergines back under the grill and cook until the sauce is only just hot and bubbling.

6. Remove from the grill and scatter over the toasted sesame seeds and spring onion. Serve immediately, with teaspoons.

Great corn

Please do not hurriedly turn the page, thinking the title of this dish refers to a chiropodist's nightmare. I mean the sunshine-yellow sweetcorn, with its frustratingly short season. Jane Baxter, one-time head of the kitchen and recipes at Riverford Organic, is one of the best cooks whose dishes I have ever had the good fortune to sample. A few years ago, at the fabulous Abergavenny food festival (I highly recommend you go – it's on the third weekend of September), she laid on a fabulous banquet one evening. The corn, served with duck, was sensational – I quite forgot my manners and scoffed far more than my fair share. This recipe is a variation on Jane's. It goes very well with roast duck or chicken. I have also eaten it with white crabmeat stirred in, and with steamed cockles and mussels.

Serves 6–8

› 6 large fat fresh corn cobs
› 100g unsalted butter
› 2 large tender onions, finely diced
› 2 teaspoons ground cumin
› 4 cloves of garlic, finely minced
› 1 small bunch of spring onions, finely sliced
› 1 1/2 teaspoons flaked sea salt
› ground black pepper

1. Remove the outer sheath from the corn and cut the kernels off the cobs, using a knife.

2. Melt the butter in a large pot and add the onions and cumin. Get them sautéing gently, as they must not be rushed and brown or burn. Cook them, stirring often, for at least 25 minutes, until golden, translucent and sticky. Add the corn.

3. Increase the heat a little and continue to cook for another 25–30 minutes, stirring often, until the corn is beginning to catch and produce a toffee-like ooze. Stir in the garlic and spring onions and cook for a further minute. Season with the sea salt and a grind of black pepper.

'The corn was sensational – I quite forgot my manners and scoffed more than my fair share.'

Grains, eggs and cheese

Green risotto

This is a favourite of mine when I want comfort with a vague element of health – the taste has a delicious vitality, as does the colour.

Serves 2

› 200g spinach leaves, watercress, small young nettles or new shoots of ground elder picked in spring, or a mixture as you see fit
› a handful of wild garlic leaves (optional)
› 2 tablespoons olive oil, plus extra for serving
› 1 stick of celery, finely diced
› 1/2 medium onion, finely diced
› 2 good fat cloves of new season's (wet) garlic or other good garlic, finely chopped
› 100g Vialone Nano risotto rice
› 100ml white wine, or 50ml vermouth
› 800ml tasty white chicken stock or vegetable stock, plus extra just-boiled water, if need be
› 40g Parmesan cheese, finely grated
› 75g fridge-cold unsalted butter, cut into cubes
› a small squeeze of fresh lemon juice (optional)
› flaked sea salt

1. Heat up a heavy shallow casserole pan with only a little water in it and collapse the greens. Drain, then rinse the leaves under cold water until cooled and wring out thoroughly. Put into a bowl and blitz with a stick blender until totally puréed. Put to one side.

2. Dry the pan and heat the oil in it. Throw in the celery and onion and sauté gently for around 10 minutes, or until tender, then add the garlic and cook for a further minute.

3. Now add the rice and gently sauté for a minute or two, stirring often. None of the pan's contents must colour. Add the wine or vermouth and let it totally evaporate.

4. Meanwhile, in another pan, bring the stock up to a simmer.

5. Start adding the hot stock to the rice, a ladle or two at a time – it should boil rapidly on entering the pan. The risotto should always be bubbling briskly and should be stirred occasionally to prevent catching and also to cream the rice starch. Don't feed with more stock until the last lot has almost gone. It will take approximately 20–25 minutes in all. If you run out of stock, use just-boiled water.

6. When the last two ladles of stock or water are in, the rice should be plump and tender but on no account chalky or mushy. Add the Parmesan and the green purée. Now drop in the cold butter and stir it in until it's melted. The risotto should become even creamier and very glossy. Season to taste with salt – a few drips of lemon juice can also be a lively addition.

7. Turn off the heat and leave to stand for a few minutes. When served, the risotto should not be too wet but should slowly migrate across the plate in a languid manner.

8. Serve with a good splash of olive oil over the top.

Penne puttanesca

This is one of my favourite pasta dishes, a particular staple of my bachelor years. There are quibbles over its origins and ingredients, but this is just time-wasting. The sauce should pack a committed punch, as it's not about subtlety. The rich oiliness and tartness from the tomato should balance the enjoyable saltiness, and the taste should be a full-on, big-hitting joy. This is not a dish for children!

Serves 4

› 3 tablespoons olive oil
› 1 small onion, very finely diced
› 50g can of anchovies in extra virgin olive oil
› 2 cloves of garlic, finely chopped
› 1/2 teaspoon dried chilli flakes
› 1/2 teaspoon dried oregano
› 2 tablespoons tomato purée
› 400g can of good chopped tomatoes
› 400g penne pasta
› 2 tablespoons baby capers, drained
› 1 large grabbing handful (around 150g) of small but interesting black and green olives, pitted and barely chopped
› grated zest of 1/2 unwaxed lemon and 1 tablespoon lemon juice
› 1 teaspoon flaked sea salt
› ground black pepper
› fresh parsley, leaves finely chopped, to garnish (optional)

1. Heat the oil in a frying pan and fry the onion for about 10 minutes, until translucent and totally soft.

2. Add the anchovies with their oil, followed by the garlic, chilli and oregano, and stir for a minute or so, or until the anchovies have collapsed and lost all shape. Add the tomato purée and cook, stirring often, until it just begins to catch and colour.

3. Flop in the canned tomatoes and let them bubble away gently until any obviously watery element to the sauce has disappeared. Neither should it resemble purée, however.

4. Meanwhile, bring a large saucepan of salted water to the boil for the pasta and drop in the penne so it will be cooked at roughly the same time as the sauce.

5. Stir the capers, olives and lemon juice into the tomato sauce and cook gently for a further 5 minutes or so.

6. Just before using the sauce, add the lemon zest. Season with the sea salt and a good grind of black pepper.

7. Drain the pasta well, then pour the sauce over it and mix well.

8. Scatter over the parsley, if using, and serve.

'The sauce should pack a committed punch – a full-on, big-hitting joy.'

Penne with chicken sauce

This is something I came across in Italy – so simple, and very pleasing indeed, as Italian cooking so often is. Made with beef or game stock instead of the chicken stock suggested here, it is also delicious. Either way, the stock needs to be good and strong. This is the kind of thing I make only for two in order to get the best results. A little synchronization is required so that the pasta and sauce are ready at the same time.

If you are making stock from the carcass of a chicken that has been roasted with a lemon inside it, see the advice on page 10 before you begin.

If using beef stock, add 1 good teaspoon of tomato purée and 50ml of red wine.

Serves 2

› 1 very large handful of fresh parsley, leaves very finely chopped
› 1 large clove of good garlic (no green shoots), very finely chopped
› finely grated zest of 1/3 unwaxed lemon
› 200g penne pasta for a generous meal, or 150g for a light meal
› 300ml fresh chicken stock
› 50ml white wine
› 40g fridge-cold unsalted butter, cut into cubes
› 10g Parmesan cheese, grated
› flaked sea salt
› ground black pepper

1. Put a saucepan of water on to boil for the penne. While it comes to the boil, make a gremolata by combining the parsley, garlic and lemon zest in a bowl. Leave to one side.

2. When the water is boiling, add the pasta with a bit of sea salt.

3. While the pasta is cooking, pour the stock and wine into a medium nonstick frying pan and briskly simmer until reduced by two-thirds, or until it appears faintly syrupy. If the reduction is ready a little earlier than expected, turn off the heat under the pan.

4. When the pasta is cooked to your liking, drain it and turn the heat back on under the chicken stock if need be.

5. Tip the pasta into the frying pan and grind over a healthy blast of black pepper. Swirl and toss the pasta over a medium high heat. Drop in 2 cubes of butter, stirring well. Continue to add the butter, 2 cubes at a time, once the previous cubes have melted. The movement will emulsify the butter with the stock, making a glossy, creamy sauce. Tip the gremolata into the pan and toss everything together well.

6. Divide the pasta between 2 plates and serve immediately with the grated Parmesan.

Peppers, beans, eggs and black pudding

This is the kind of shoestring dinner I rely on when really trying not to go food shopping.

Serves 2

> 2 red romano peppers
> 100g fresh or frozen broad beans
> 1 small onion, halved and very finely sliced
> 1 tablespoon olive oil, plus extra for frying
> 40g unsalted butter
> 1 small clove of good hard garlic, crushed
> about 1 tablespoon sherry vinegar
> 100g good black pudding or morcilla, cut into 4 slices, each around 2cm thick
> 10g fresh parsley leaves, chopped
> 2 free-range eggs
> smoked paprika
> flaked sea salt

1. If you have a gas hob, turn it on and place the peppers directly over the flame, moving them around until totally charcoal black and blistered all over. Alternatively this can be done under the grill.

2. Allow the peppers to cool before rubbing their charred skin away from the flesh with your thumb or a little kitchen paper. Do not rinse off the skin under water, as the peppers will lose their lovely charred taste. Deseed the peppers thoroughly, then tear them into strips lengthways.

3. While the peppers char, quickly boil the beans for 4–5 minutes or so or until tender. Rinse under cold water and, unless they are really young, peel them from their jackets.

4. In a smallish saucepan, preferably nonstick, gently cook the onion in the oil and half the butter until it turns totally soft and golden, about 10 minutes.

5. Stir in the peppers, followed by enough sea salt to bring out their taste, and the garlic.

6. Tip in just enough vinegar to give the peppers and onion a definite sweet and sharp edge but not to overpower them. Continue to cook until the vinegar has totally evaporated, then remove the pan from the heat.

7. Heat a little oil in a small frying pan and start to fry the black pudding or morcilla until slightly crispy on the outside but warm and moist within.

8. Chop the remaining butter into little lumps and drop it into the peppers and onion. Stir in the beans and parsley and check the seasoning once more, then add the black pudding and keep warm.

9. Meanwhile, fry the eggs in a separate pan.

10. Serve the eggs on 2 plates, alongside the black pudding mixture, and sprinkle the egg yolks with smoked paprika.

Herb omelette

So often I hear the words, 'I don't have the time to cook.' Yes, you do, we all do and if you don't, then how come? The internet is fizzing with suggestions, and there are enough cookbooks out there to stack and build a town called Epicuria. There is no end of ideas for dishes to suit any size of window in our diary schedule or daily grind (good name for a coffee shop). So all those who don't have time to cook even this humble omelette and sit down with a glass of wine, I worry for you.

Some notes: First, I was always taught that an omelette should not be well browned – if, in fact, at all. Second, most houses do not have a small omelette pan with steep curved sides which allows you to jerk and roll the omelette into a cocoon without touching it. An omelette is a very personal thing and if you like a little colour on yours, that's fine, as is folding it with a spatula. I would say, however, that a good omelette must be a little runny in the middle, otherwise the fun has been tortured from it. In the UK we view barely cooked eggs as some kind of deadly sin. WRONG?

Serves 1

> 2 free-range eggs
> 1 tablespoon cream
> a generous pinch of flaked sea salt
> 2 sprigs of fresh tarragon, leaves picked off and roughly chopped
> 1 bushy sprig of fresh dill, roughly chopped
> 2 sprigs of tender young fresh parsley, leaves finely chopped
> a few fresh chives, finely chopped
> 40g unsalted butter
> a small splash of sunflower oil

1. Beat the eggs in a bowl with the cream, sea salt and half the herbs.

2. Heat the butter with the oil in a small nonstick or well-sealed frying pan. When the fat is very hot, tip in the eggs and allow them to sit in the pan for 10 seconds or so, until the base of the omelette is just set.

3. Tip in the remaining herbs, tilt the pan away from you at about 45 degrees and, with a sharp little shovelling motion, roll and jerk the omelette back on itself. Holding the pan above the heat and every now and then putting it directly back on it, repeat until the omelette is totally rolled. Otherwise flip it with a spatula when appropriate. When the omelette is done, the ends should not be leaking but a slight press should let you know that the middle is a little runny. The whole process should take approximately 2$\frac{1}{2}$ minutes.

4. Tip the omelette on to a plate and eat immediately with a nice little French-dressed salad and a glass of white wine.

Eggs and tapenade

Whether they are enjoyed on a picnic with celery salt, sliced into a Spanish café salad, piped with mayonnaise in Paris, hoiked from a bulbous jar of vinegar in a dark pub, or found rattling around the inside of a Scotch egg, bring me more hard-boiled eggs. I had a bowl of tapenade left over and decided that hard-boiled eggs would be good vehicles to finish it with. I was right. This tapenade, although easy to make, uses a few more ingredients than more humble versions.

Do not use the totally tasteless, cheap black olives with an immaculate hole. They are green olives uniformly oxidized to turn black. If different varieties are loose and on display, taste them, but choose some that have not been ruined with all sorts of herbs, chilli, lemon peel, stale garlic or too much salt.

Serves 4

› 8 only just hard-boiled free-range eggs (the yolks should be moist but not runny)

For the tapenade
› 150g good black olives, pitted and chopped as fine as is possible by hand
› $1/2$ teaspoon dried thyme or rosemary, rubbed to dust
› 6 good salted brown anchovies in oil, chopped and mushed to a purée
› 10g fresh parsley, very finely chopped
› 1 heaped tablespoon finely grated Parmesan cheese
› 2 small cloves of very good hard garlic (no green shoots), very finely mushed
› 1 heaped teaspoon Dijon mustard
› a squeeze of fresh lemon juice, enough to put in a presence but not take over the show
› a small pinch of dried chilli flakes, to taste
› 2 tablespoons extra virgin olive oil

1. Combine all the ingredients for the tapenade, beating in the oil at the end. Place in a bowl.

2. Serve the eggs in their shells, as it's nice to tap and peel them while talking and drinking a cold bottle of Albariño.

3. Put the tapenade alongside, with knives for halving the eggs and spreading the tapenade.

American egg

I have no idea why my dad referred to this as an American egg – we never got to the bottom of it. He just told me that this was what it was called when he was a child. I guess the fact that my grandmother was a formidable American lady from Maine could help with the mystery of the naming. Anyway, it always made us laugh when we made it together, because there's quite a lot of pain involved in its preparation as the shells are peeled from the eggs while they are still hot. It's really just a soft-boiled egg chopped up, with the added joy of eating it from a teacup with a luxuriously big knob of butter and some chives stirred in.

By the way, if Oscar Meyer American bacon is available from your supermarket, buy some and cook it until totally crisp – it's a good accompaniment and I guess makes these eggs closer to their dubious origin.

Serves 1

› 2 free-range eggs, at room temperature
› 25g unsalted butter
› 2 teaspoons finely chopped fresh chives
› flaked sea salt
› ground black pepper
› hot buttered white toast, to serve

1. Drop the eggs into a small saucepan of boiling water. Boil for $4^{1}/2$ minutes, or until the white is only just cooked and the yolk is still runny. We all have our own methods for achieving this. Delia would suggest boiling for 1 minute with no lid, then taking the eggs off the heat, putting a lid on and leaving them for a further 4 minutes.

2. Take the eggs from the water and tap all over on a hard surface so that the shells are thoroughly broken, using cold running water to cool your fingers down when the pain gets too much. Peel the eggs as quickly as possible and drop them into a teacup.

3. Chop the butter into little cubes and drop them into the cup too. Take a knife and slice repeatedly through the eggs until all is combined.

4. Scatter in the chives, add a good pinch of sea salt and a generous grind of black pepper, and enjoy with the toast that you remembered to synchronize with the serving of the eggs.

Dal

This dish saw me through my student days, as it's pretty cheap to make. There are so many recipes for dal, all giving or taking some of the things you will see here. Don't get hung up on not having the more unusual ingredients. I've written 'optional' next to those that don't matter as much. I like my dal quite wet, anything stiffer reminding me of annoying 'right-on' cafés employing arrogant staff who are not quite as 'peaceful' or 'chilled' as they profess. If the peas are not easy to find in the supermarket (though they should be), try your local health-food shop. Ghee is very easy to buy these days. It is tempting, I know, to chuck everything in at the beginning, but layering is needed so that everything does what it should.

Asafoetida is made from the dried and ground root of a relative to fennel. Although pungent to the point where it is also called stink gum, it is a staple ingredient in a dal, really boosting the flavour. A lot of the larger supermarkets now sell it.

I eat my dal with naan picked up from the takeaway on the way home, as the bagged supermarket brands are, generally speaking, pretty bad and I've never made it from scratch.

Serves 3–4

- › 75g ghee or unsalted butter
- › 1 teaspoon black mustard seeds (optional)
- › 1 teaspoon cumin seeds
- › 15 fresh curry leaves (optional but advisable)
- › 1 red onion, medium diced
- › ½ cinnamon stick
- › 4 cloves of good garlic, finely sliced
- › 50g fresh ginger, peeled and finely grated
- › 1 tablespoon finely chopped fresh coriander stalks
- › 1 hot long green chilli, quartered
- › 2 teaspoons ground turmeric
- › 1 teaspoon ground asafoetida (optional)
- › 250g dried yellow split peas
- › 1.5–1.7 litres cold water
- › 100ml coconut milk
- › 2 teaspoons flaked sea salt
- › naan bread, to serve

1. Put a wok or medium saucepan over a medium heat and add the ghee. Tip in the mustard seeds, if using, and cumin. Stir or swirl often. When the mustard seeds start to dance and pop and their lovely toasted smell comes to the nose they and the cumin are done.

2. Now add the curry leaves, if using, and stir them around for 30 seconds or so. They should also make a popping sound as they blister. Add the onion and cinnamon stick and allow the onion to sauté, stirring often, until evenly and well browned all over – about 16–18 minutes.

3. Add the garlic and continue to fry until the onion is a little darker and the garlic is golden. Stir in the ginger, coriander, chilli, turmeric and asafoetida, if using, and continue to cook for a further 30 seconds or so, stirring all the time.

4. Tip in the split peas, immediately followed by the water. Bring up to a healthy simmer and cook for approximately 1 hour, or until the peas are tender and collapsing. If you feel you need a bit more water, add it as necessary. The dal should be wet and creamy, as you would expect to find pouring double cream, but not watery, so continue to cook until it has the right consistency.

5. Add the coconut milk 20 minutes before the cooking time is up.

6. Add the sea salt – a fair amount is needed to bring out the full flavour properly – and serve with naan bread.

Henry's lentil and quail's egg salad

One of my favourite restaurants is Racine, which is nestled among the shops along the Brompton Road in London. Henry Harris, the chef and owner, is a good friend of mine and a very fine cook, to say the least. Here is one of my favourites from his extensive repertoire of what he calls his 'good bourgeois food'. The anchovy dressing recipe makes more than you will need, but is excellent for a Caesar-style salad or even drizzled over pork, lamb or veal chops. It will keep for 3 days in the fridge. Quails' eggs are delicate little things that at times resist peeling and break up, so it is worth doing a few extra in case you lose a couple whilst peeling.

Serves 4-ish

> 150g Puy lentils
> 1 bay leaf
> 12–18 quail's eggs
> a good glug of red or white wine vinegar
> a generous handful of fresh flat-leaf parsley
> 1 tablespoon finely chopped shallot
> 4 tablespoons olive oil
> juice of 1/2 lemon, plus extra if needed
> flaked sea salt
> ground black pepper
> 4 very nice salted anchovy fillets (try the Ortíz brand, from Spain), to garnish

For the anchovy dressing

> 50g can of salted anchovies in olive oil
> 2 free-range egg yolks
> 2 cloves of garlic, crushed
> 1 teaspoon English mustard
> 2 teaspoons Worcestershire sauce
> 1 teaspoon Tabasco
> juice of 1 small lemon
> 300ml olive oil

1. Soak the lentils in a bowl of cold water for 24 hours, then drain.

2. Put the lentils into a saucepan with the bay leaf, cover with fresh water and bring to a gentle simmer. Cook for 30–40 minutes, or until tender. Remove from the heat, season with sea salt and pepper and let cool.

3. Bring a good-sized saucepan of water to the boil with 1 teaspoon sea salt. Prick the round end of each quail's egg with a pin and cook them for exactly 1 minute and 40 seconds, in batches of 6. Lift the eggs from the pan and place them in a bowl of iced water to chill rapidly. Throw the vinegar into the bowl and leave for an hour. Then carefully peel the eggs and put them into another bowl of cold water.

4. Hold the parsley tightly together against a chopping board and cut it into fine strips. Drain the lentils and transfer them to a mixing bowl along with the parsley, shallot, olive oil and lemon juice. Mix well and season with sea salt, pepper and more lemon if needed.

5. To make the anchovy dressing, place all the ingredients except for the olive oil in a tall beaker and blitz to a purée with an electric hand blender, or use a liquidizer. Drizzle in the olive oil in a thin, steady stream and whiz to make a good, tight dressing. If it gets too thick, thin it down with some cold water. You want it to have the consistency of a thick pouring cream. Check the seasoning and adjust the spice or acidity as desired.

6. Spoon the lentil salad into 4 soup plates or similar and place 3 or 4 eggs on top of each pile. Drizzle over a few tablespoons of the anchovy dressing and garnish with an anchovy fillet and a good grinding of black pepper.

Couscous salad

The point here is that the couscous should be swarming with treats and colours. You shouldn't be having to inspect little flecks as if they infiltrated via a messy cook. This is great served with barbecued lamb.

› 1 medium cucumber, peeled, deseeded and finely diced
› 2 teaspoons flaked sea salt, plus extra to season
› around 500ml sunflower oil or light olive oil, for frying
› 2 small onions, halved and sliced paper thin
› 150g quick-cook couscous
› 3 tablespoons olive oil
› 50g green sultanas (or failing that, golden or standard ones)
› 250ml boiling water
› 80g shelled pistachio nuts
› 50g shelled walnuts, broken up
› 4 large vine tomatoes, deseeded and medium diced
› 1 medium red onion, finely diced
› 50g dried barberries (optional)
› 40g sour cherries, roughly but fairly finely chopped
› 35g fresh mint, leaves roughly chopped
› 50g fresh parsley, leaves finely chopped
› 35g fresh dill, fronds roughly chopped
› 2 large handfuls of good, wrinkly, salty, little black olives, pitted
› finely grated zest of 1 medium unwaxed lemon and juice of 1/2 lemon
› ground black pepper
› 1/4 teaspoon ground cinnamon, to garnish

1. Mix the cucumber with the sea salt and tip into a colander set over a bowl. Leave to drain for 30 minutes.

2. Meanwhile pour the sunflower or light olive oil into a saucepan (it should be about 2.5cm deep) and fry the onions over a medium heat, moving them often, for 1 1/2–2 minutes until golden brown. Remove the onions with a slotted spoon and drain on kitchen paper. They should be totally crisp. Rule: not crispy = not fun; burnt = not fun.

3. Tip the couscous into a heatproof bowl and rub in 1 tablespoon of the olive oil. Stir in the sultanas, then pour over the boiling water, give the couscous a good stir and cover with a tea towel held down with a plate. Leave to sit for 5 minutes, or until the water has been absorbed.

4. While it is still warm, break up the couscous with a fork and stir in the rest of the olive oil. Season with sea salt. Tip into a large serving bowl and allow to come to room temperature.

5. Toast the nuts in a dry frying pan over a medium–high heat until golden, taking care not to burn them. Transfer them to a plate to cool.

6. Add all the goodies except the fried onions and cinnamon to the couscous and mix well. Check the seasoning.

7. Scatter a very light dusting of cinnamon over the top of the couscous, then sprinkle over the crispy onions.

Baked Vacherin Mont d'Or with accompaniments

This is the heartiest of winter comfort food and has me wishing for cold weather. Although tempting, don't eat this all by yourself; you will feel sick!

Serves 4

› 1 Vacherin Mont d'Or cheese
› 2 large cloves of garlic, finely sliced (optional)
› 1 large sprig of fresh rosemary, leaves picked (optional)
› 4 new potatoes or 2 Pink Fir Apple potatoes per person
› 8 good fresh spring onions
› 4 large gherkins (not the sweet, cured type)
› 1 head of chicory
› a good sourdough stick
› flaked sea salt
› ground black pepper

1. Prior to baking the cheese, remove it from its box and soak the box in warm water for at least 30 minutes, or until sodden. Discard any paper that may be wrapped around the cheese.

2. Preheat the oven to 200°C/ fan 180°C/gas 6.

3. If using the garlic or rosemary, make 10 incisions in the top of the cheese. Push slivers of garlic into half of them and rosemary leaves into the other half, not pushing them all the way in. Remove the box from the water and put the cheese back in it.

4. Bring a large saucepan of water to the boil. Drop in the potatoes and only then put the cheese on a baking tray and into the oven to bake for 15 minutes.

5. Arrange the spring onions, gherkins and some whole chicory leaves around the edge of a large chopping board, leaving room in the centre for the baked cheese.

6. Drain the potatoes and put them into a bowl. Season them with sea salt and pepper.

7. Put the cheese in the middle of the board and take both the board and bowl of potatoes to the table with a loaf of bread (preferably a good sourdough stick). Remember to cut out the rind from the top face of the cheese before getting involved with a spoon. Eat the cheese with all the accompaniments.

'This is the heartiest of winter comfort food.'

Mozzarella and roast endive salad

When I was working for Alastair Little we made some great salads, and this was a particular favourite of mine. I'm not a fan of rocket or balsamic vinegar, but here they both work brilliantly.

Serves 4

› 2 tablespoons pine nuts
› 2 endives or red endives (trevise)
› 25g unsalted butter
› 1 tablespoon good balsamic vinegar, plus extra for drizzling
› 1 teaspoon caster sugar
› 1 tablespoon fresh lemon juice
› 1 tablespoon extra virgin olive oil, plus extra for drizzling
› a small pinch of dried chilli flakes
› a small handful of rocket leaves
› 2 really good mozzarella balls or 1 burrata, drained
› flaked sea salt
› ground black pepper

1. Preheat the oven to 190°C/fan 170°C/gas 5.

2. Put the pine nuts into a small saucepan and swirl over a medium heat continuously until they take on a nice golden colour. Tip them out of the pan to cool, as they will burn if you don't.

3. Take one of the endives and remove any damaged outside leaves. When removing the stalk end, it's essential that you cut off only a thin slice so that you keep the leaves connected to the core. Quarter the endive lengthways, then cut each quarter in half lengthways (or into thirds if the endive is a large one).

4. Lay the cut endive on a baking sheet lined with baking parchment. Melt the butter in a small saucepan and paint the endive heavily with about half the butter. Sprinkle with sea salt.

5. Put the endive into the oven and cook for about 15–20 minutes. Turn the endive pieces over and paint the undersides with the rest of the butter, then put them back into the oven for another 15 minutes, or until the leaves are almost beginning to burn. Splash them with the balsamic vinegar and sprinkle with the sugar, and then continue to cook until the leaves are brown and crispy. The stem should be a combination of off-white and browned. Take the endive out of the oven when done and allow to cool fully.

6. Put the lemon juice, olive oil and dried chilli into a large bowl and whisk with a fork. Snap the leaves from the remaining raw endive, and add them to the bowl of dressing. Add the rocket leaves and toss together.

7. Tear the mozzarella balls in half or your burrata into quarters and put in the centre of 4 serving plates. Season with a little sea salt and black pepper. Arrange the fresh salad around the cheese, having flicked any excess dressing back into the bowl – less is more, from a visual perspective.

8. Arrange the roasted endive over the mozzarella and salad – it looks better if bent and open rather than straight. Wave a few streaks of balsamic vinegar over everything, add a last streak of olive oil and finally scatter over the pine nuts.

Cheese, leek and potato pie

I don't make pies often but I absolutely love them. Rarely does this one make it past one day. After the initial slice I wrap up the rest with rationing in mind, but it's pointless, really, with trips back to the pie at intervals of every 5 or 10 minutes. This is simple stuff, a good thing, as generally speaking life's too complicated. More cheese and potato pie, please, and less ballotine of rabbit with crayfish mousseline, cocoa foam gel and pine needle mist.

Please feel free to slip some ham in between the potato layers. And sometimes an urgent enthusiasm for pie calls for pre-made pastry.

Serves 2 (doubles well, to serve 4–6)

› 50g unsalted butter
› 3 large leeks, sliced (700g prepared weight)
› 1 Braeburn apple, peeled, cored and coarsely grated
› 1/2 teaspoon flaked sea salt
› 1/2 teaspoon grated nutmeg
› 225g medium Maris Piper potatoes, peeled and grated
› 140g mature Cheddar cheese, coarsely grated
› 500g ready-made shortcrust pastry
› plain flour, for dusting
› 2 good tablespoons wholegrain mustard
› 1 free-range egg
› 1 tablespoon milk
› ground black pepper

1. Preheat the oven to 190°C/fan 170°C/gas 5 and line a baking tray with baking parchment.

2. Melt the butter in a frying pan, throw in the leeks and cook over a medium heat, stirring often to prevent burning, for approximately 18 minutes, until totally tender and moist but not wet. Add the apple and season with the sea salt, nutmeg and a very good grind of black pepper. Allow to cool. Warm will do.

3. Add the potatoes to the leeks. Fold them in, then follow with the 125g of the Cheddar.

4. Divide the pastry in half. Take one piece and roll it into a ball. Flatten the ball and place it on a lightly floured surface. Roll into a 26cm disc, turning frequently to keep the pastry as round as possible. Using a 25cm dinner plate or cake tin as a guide, cut out a neat circle. Place the circle of pastry on the prepared baking tray.

5. Smear 1 tablespoon of the mustard over the centre of the pastry, leaving a 2cm border all the way around. Top with the cooked leeks and potatoes, heaping them up in the centre. Beat the egg with the milk and brush very lightly around the border of the filled pastry circle.

6. Roll out and cut the remaining pastry in the same way as the first half. Lay the pastry circle over the filling and press the edges neatly on to the lower base. The filling should be snug inside. Don't rush. Crimp the edges.

7. Paint the whole pie, top, sides and crimped border, with the egg and milk mixture and scatter over the remaining Cheddar. Poke a small hole in the pie top and bake in the oven for 1 hour.

8. Allow to cool a bit, then storm it.

Tomato and goats' cheese salad

This is the kind of thing I enjoy for a perfect little lunch, not the heavy, slowing thing it so often can be.

Serves 4

> › 14 Unctuous Slow-roasted Tomatoes (*see* page 147)
> › 1/4 teaspoon dried chilli flakes
> › 1 tub of soft fresh rindless sheep's or goats' curd or cheese
> › grated zest and juice of 1 unwaxed lemon
> › 24 Kalamata olives, pitted
> › 1/2 red onion, very finely sliced
> › a small bunch of fresh flat-leaf parsley, roughly chopped
> › extra virgin olive oil

1. Arrange half the tomatoes on a plate and sprinkle over a little of the chilli, some pieces of curd or cheese, and half the lemon zest, olives and onion. Add another layer of tomatoes and repeat the sprinkling, then scatter over the parsley.

2. Dress with extra virgin olive oil and lemon juice.

'...the kind of thing I enjoy for a perfect little lunch.'

Pommes aligot

The first time I had this was outside Clermont-Ferrand, northerly positioned in France's Massif Central. I had never heard of this potato dish, and my friend Xavier had planned an evening for me specifically to go and eat it. Washed down with lots of wine, it made me swoon. Tomme de Cantal cheese, cream and garlic are beaten into boiled and riced potato, leaving it soft like a purée but with a beautiful, mozzarella-like, stretching consistency. In a luxurious manner it just furtively oozes: 'Eat me.'

This heavenly potato dish is often served alongside garlic sausage. Red wine is essential to help your stomach deal with the elasticity of the cheese. The garlic must be excellent – it can be added raw or boiled with the potatoes.

Serves 2–4

› 400g floury potatoes, peeled
› 3 cloves of good hard garlic, peeled but left whole
› 1 teaspoon flaked sea salt, plus extra to season
› 50g unsalted butter
› 150ml double cream
› 250g Tomme de Cantal or Wigmore cheese, rind removed and discarded, grated

1. Submerge the potatoes and garlic in a large saucepan of cold water. Add the sea salt and bring to the boil. Cook for approximately 20 minutes, or until the potatoes are totally tender, then drain thoroughly, making sure the garlic cloves remain with the potatoes.

2. Mash the potatoes and garlic in the pan. Ideally you will use a ricer or mouli, but if using a masher, it's especially important to make sure the potatoes are thoroughly cooked so as to avoid lumps.

3. Return the pan to a medium heat and beat in the butter and cream, then stir in the cheese. Beat to incorporate, making sure it is all lovely and hot and melted. Check the seasoning and add extra sea salt if need be.

4. Serve piping hot, either on its own or with garlic sausage.

'In a luxurious manner this just furtively oozes: "Eat me."'

Quiche Lorraine

Quiche is so often dismissed as a relic, that soggy-bottomed misery served to visitors queuing tray-in-hand in the café of a country pile full of dusty armour and equally dusty wardens. That's English quiche, though, full of knackered broccoli or grisly trimmings of smoked salmon, and, yes, we have a lot to answer for.

I have to thank that genius novelist, cook and artist Len Deighton here, as it was while leafing through his *Action Cookbook* researching '60s food that quiche Lorraine was bought back into my consciousness. It is a simple classic delight that should not be tampered with, and this recipe showcases quiche as the great dish it is.

Serves 6

> plain flour, for dusting
> 500g ready-made shortcrust pastry
> 150g smoked bacon lardons or smoked ham
> 1 teaspoon sunflower oil
> 3 large free-range eggs, plus 1 egg yolk
> 150g Gruyère cheese, grated
> 400ml double cream
> 3 tablespoons crème fraîche
> a scratch of nutmeg
> ground black pepper

1. Preheat the oven to 200°C/fan 180°C/gas 6.

2. On a lightly floured surface, roll out the pastry to a thickness of about 3mm. Line a 23cm springform tart tin with the pastry, but do not trim the excess. There must be no holes, otherwise the tart will leak and this is bad for morale and the bottom of your oven. Make sure the pastry is pushed into the curved corner of the tin and snug against the sides. Leave the overhang.

3. Transfer the tart tin to a baking tray. Cover the pastry case with baking parchment you have scrumpled up and reopened (it will fit better). Pour in some baking weights, or use beans or rice, remembering to keep them for this task in future rather than waste them in the bin.

4. Cook the pastry case until golden (about 25 minutes), and in the meantime gently fry the bacon lardons or smoked ham in the oil until only just beginning to colour. Drain on kitchen paper.

5. Remove the pastry case from the oven and the paper from the pastry. Brush the pastry all over the bottom and inner sides with one of the eggs, beaten. Cook for a further 6 minutes, without covering. Remove from the oven and reduce the oven temperature to 180°C/fan 160°/gas 4.

6. Scatter the lardons or ham all over the bottom of the tart case, followed by the cheese.

7. Beat together the remaining 2 eggs and the egg yolk with the cream, crème fraîche, a grinding of black pepper and a little scratch of nutmeg. Pour the mixture into the pastry case and return to the oven for a further 30–35 minutes. When you think it's ready, jiggle the tray. The middle of the tart should not be set too hard and should wobble ever so slightly. Remove the tart from the oven and let it rest for 15 minutes or so.

8. Snap or cut off the overhanging pastry from the tart, then, using a cloth so as not to burn your fingertips, push the tart on its base out of the ring and transfer it to a board.

9. Serve warm, with a good French-dressed salad that has been garnished with a few chives.

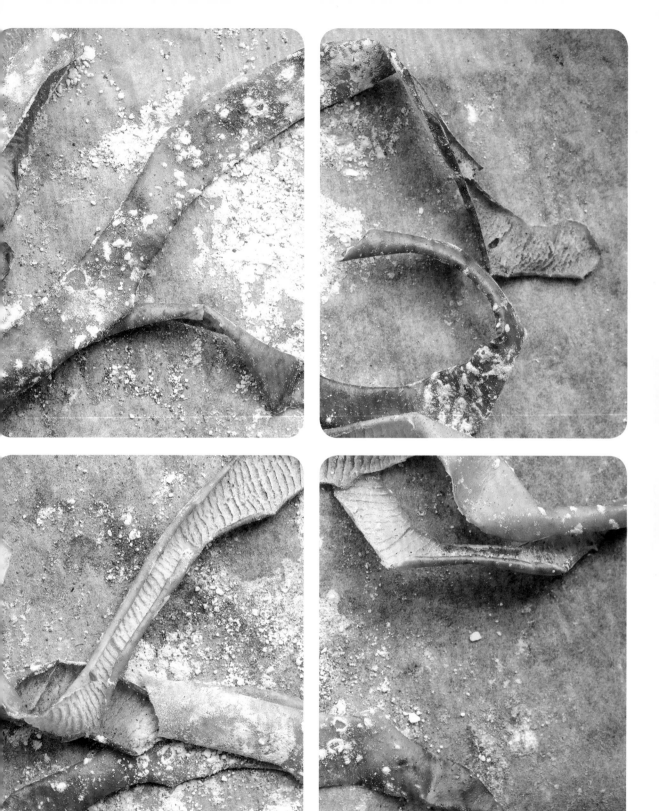

Puddings

Pink grapefruit and Campari granita

Campari with pink grapefruit juice is a favourite early evening drink of mine so I thought an iced version could only be a good idea – 'same same but different'.

Serves 4-6

› 400ml freshly squeezed and strained ruby grapefruit juice (approx. 3 grapefruits)
› 75ml Campari
› 50ml freshly squeezed and strained lemon juice
› 3 tablespoons caster sugar

1. Stir the grapefruit juice, Campari, lemon juice and sugar together in a measuring jug or bowl until the sugar has totally dissolved.

2. Strain into a freezerproof container. Attach the lid and pop into the freezer for 2 hours.

3. Distress the freshly frozen liquid, scraping it with a fork, and continue to do this every 1–2 hours until you have a snow-like consistency.

4. Spoon the granita into chilled glasses and serve immediately.

Passion fruit ice cream

Passion fruits are something I never remember to eat enough of, but I have a clear memory of buying a crammed binliner full of them on the side of a motorway in Kenya for the equivalent of 40p in 1995. I can only imagine the astonished face of the seller if I'd told him what a single passion fruit would cost at home. This ice cream is for special occasions as the fruits are expensive.

I leave a quarter of the seeds in the juice, as I like the crunch.

Serves 6–8

› 16 big passion fruits
› 200ml full-fat milk
› 400ml double cream
› 6 free-range egg yolks
› 100g sugar

1. Halve 4 of the passion fruits and scoop out the seeds and flesh into a bowl. Place a sieve over the bowl and scoop the seeds and flesh from the remaining passion fruits into the sieve. Press down hard on the seeds and flesh with a ladle to release as much of the juice and pulp into the bowl as possible – be persistent.

2. Heat the milk and cream together in a large saucepan until it only just starts to boil.

3. In the meantime, beat the egg yolks with the sugar until pale and very creamy.

4. Pour the heated milk and cream mixture into the bowl of eggs and sugar, whisking all the time. Pour the contents of the bowl back into the saucepan and tip in the passion fruit juice.

5. Put the saucepan over a low heat and stir constantly, taking care to work the spoon into the corners and over the bottom of the pan and paying attention all the time – the minute you notice the mixture starting to thicken to runny custard, you must take it off the heat. (Any more cooking and the mixture will resemble scrambled eggs.)

6. Pour the mixture straight into the container you plan to freeze it in and let it cool completely. If the mixture has scrambled but only slightly, you can pass it through a strainer into the container. This will remove the seeds as well as the clots. But better some ice cream than no ice cream.

7. Put a lid on the container and place it in the freezer. Stir the contents vigorously every 1½ hours. This will become more difficult as the ice cream becomes harder. Keep doing this until the ice cream is set.

8. Take the ice cream out of the freezer for a few minutes before serving, as this will make it easier to scoop.

Rice pudding with sour cherry sauce

Trine Hahnemann, a friend and famous Danish cook, had been helping me research a series on Scandinavian food. One day, while leafing through her excellent book *The Scandinavian Cook*, I saw that she put fresh cherry compote on her cold rice pudding. Here I have used sharp little dried sour cherries in place of fresh. Thank you, Trine, and I hope you don't mind my meddling.

Serves 4–6

› 200g pudding rice
› 1 litre full-fat milk
› 2 bay leaves
› 1 vanilla pod, split and seeds scraped out
› 80g soft brown sugar
› 150ml double cream
› ½ whole nutmeg, finely grated

For the sour cherry sauce
› 100g dried sour cherries
› 3 tablespoons cherry brandy, brandy or cognac (or cold water)
› 1 teaspoon cornflour
› 3 tablespoons cherry jam, ideally morello
› 2–3 teaspoons fresh lemon juice

1. To make the sour cherry sauce, put the cherries and cherry brandy, cognac or water into a saucepan with 200ml cold water and bring to a gentle simmer. Cook for 5 minutes, or until the cherries look swollen, stirring occasionally.

2. Next, mix the cornflour with 1 tablespoon cold water in a small bowl. Add this to the cherries with the jam and cook over a low heat for 2–3 minutes, until the sauce is thickened and glossy.

3. Stir in the lemon juice to taste. The sauce should taste slightly sour, to cut through the sweetness and creaminess of the rice. Pour into a heatproof jug and leave to cool, then cover and chill. The sauce will continue to thicken as it cools.

4. Put the rice into a large nonstick saucepan and add the milk, bay leaves, vanilla seeds and sugar. Bring up to a simmer and continue to cook for the next 20 minutes or so, until the rice is just tender, stirring occasionally and more frequently towards the end to prevent it sticking and burning.

5. Remove the bay leaves and stir the cream and nutmeg into the rice.

6. Eat immediately with the cold cherry sauce spooned over the top.

Baked peaches with amaretto and almonds

Old-school? Too right! I will do my best to keep this pudding from disappearing into obscurity. 'A bit *Abigail's Party*,' you may sneer. 'Maybe so,' I will reply, 'but delicious none the less.' Often the biscuits are used as a kind of replacement stone or as a crumble topping for the peaches but I find that, when baked, they go soggy. Therefore I have put them into the cream instead.

Serves 6

› 75g unsalted butter, plus extra for greasing
› 3 just-ripe peaches, halved and stones removed
› 100ml amaretto liqueur
› 6 teaspoons soft brown sugar
› juice of 1/2 lemon
› 8 amaretti biscuits
› finely grated zest of 1 unwaxed orange
› 300ml pouring double cream
› toasted flaked almonds, to decorate

1. Preheat the oven to 200°C/fan 180°C/gas 6.

2. Lightly grease the bottom of an ovenproof dish and put in the peach halves, flat-side up. Over the face of each peach and into each cavity liberally splash a good amount of amaretto.

3. Now divide the butter into 6 slices and put a slice on top of each peach. Sprinkle 1 teaspoon brown sugar on top of each peach half. Finally squeeze a dribble of lemon juice over each half.

4. Put the peaches into the oven and bake them for 30 minutes, depending on their ripeness. They want to be soft but just holding their form.

5. In the meantime, crumble the amaretti biscuits into coarse crumbs with your hands.

6. Add the orange zest to the cream, then whip it until it forms semi-stiff peaks. Fold the biscuit crumbs into the cream and decorate it with the toasted flaked almonds.

7. Remove the peaches from the oven and allow them to cool a bit, then serve with the biscuit cream.

'Old-school? Too right! I will do my best to keep this pudding from disappearing into obscurity.'

Frank's mother-in-law's friend's syrup sponge

Despite the cooking time, this recipe is a doddle that delivers hearty feel-good results. Prepare it, then, 2 hours before pudding, put it on the hob, set the timer, and turn your attention to other things.

Lord Francis runs the Glynde Food and English Wine Festival in East Sussex. I went to his house for a family lunch one rainy weekend and this was served alongside a jug of double cream and another containing hot syrup. The pudding basin was pleasingly large, but that didn't stop us seeing off the sponge inside apart from one bite, left unfinished and lonely on the plate. Everyone declined this last mouthful, which in hindsight was idiotic considering the gluttony that had preceded it. For goodness' sake, if there is ever a forkful, a crumb or a smear left behind, show some respect and please, someone, just take responsibility and finish it. I will do the same.

Serves about 4 adults and 5 children (ie lunch at ours)

> 3 free-range eggs
> the same weight as the eggs in their shell of unsalted butter, plus some for greasing the basin
> the same weight as the eggs in their shells of caster sugar
> grated zest of 1 small unwaxed lemon or 1/2 unwaxed orange, finely grated (both optional)
> the same weight as the eggs in their shells of self-raising flour
> a pinch of flaked sea salt
> 454g can of golden syrup
> pouring double cream, to serve

1. Cream the butter and sugar together in a mixing bowl, using an electric whisk. Break in the eggs and add the zest (if using). Beat to combine. Once combined, the mixture may look curdled, but this doesn't seem to matter in the end.

2. Sift the flour and sea salt into the bowl, then, with the motor on slow, whiz until only just folded in. (Blend too long or too fast and the pudding won't rise as well.)

3. Take a 1-litre pudding basin and smear butter thoroughly around its interior. Put 2 very generous dessertspoons golden syrup into the bottom of the basin.

4. Pour the thick batter mix over the syrup and level it out.

5. Seal the basin with clingfilm in a slightly baggy fashion, followed by a length of tin foil with a neat pleat in the middle.

6. Put the basin on to a trivet or upturned saucer in the bottom of a large, lidded saucepan. Pour in about 8cm of water and bring it up to the boil, then put the lid on and cook the pudding for 2 hours, adding more water when needed.

7. When just about to serve, heat the remaining syrup in a small pan and pour it into a jug.

8. Loosen the pudding from the basin by running a thin sharp knife around the edge, then upend it on to a plate.

9. Serve with lashings of the warmed golden syrup and double cream. How is it possible to have too much of a good thing?

Pancakes with chestnut sauce

I will never decline anything that involves chestnuts.

Makes 6 small pancakes

> 100g plain flour
> 1 large free-range egg
> 200ml full-fat milk
> unsalted butter, for frying
> flaked sea salt
> icing sugar, sifted, to serve

For the chestnut sauce

> 415g can of chestnut purée
> 2 tablespoons full-fat milk
> 100ml double cream
> about 2–3 teaspoons dark runny honey, to taste
> 1–2 tablespoons brandy (optional)

1. Sift the flour into a bowl and add a pinch of salt to stop the pancakes themselves being bland. Add the egg and half the milk and beat together with vigour, so as to remove any lumps, until you have a smooth batter. Beat in the rest of the milk. Put the batter into the fridge to chill for at least 30 minutes.

2. To make the chestnut sauce, tip the chestnut purée into a small saucepan over a moderate heat and add the milk and cream. Stir well until the ingredients have combined and bring the mixture to a gentle simmer.

3. Now add the honey until the mixture is as sweet as you desire. Add the brandy, if using.

4. Pop a little butter into a medium–smallish frying pan. Pour approximately 2 generous tablespoons of the batter into the pan, immediately swirling, so that the batter thinly coats the bottom of the pan. Cook over a medium–low heat for about 2 minutes, until the pancake is golden brown on the underside.

5. Flip the pancake with a fish slice or toss it on to its other side with a palette knife, and then cook until golden brown. Slide the pancake on to a plate. Spread a generous 2 tablespoonfuls of the chestnut sauce across the bottom of the pancake, then fold over and fold again. Dust with plenty of icing sugar and attack.

6. If you want to cook all the pancakes first, stack them on a plate and keep them in a warm oven until the last one has been cooked, then fill them and eat them in one batch.

Cheat's ginger pudding

Having delayed homecoming with a pint or two I really didn't have time for, then trying to cook, clear up the house, lay the table, bath, change and look calm, I inevitably call on this pudding. I'll probably have to dash to the shops for the cake, having not picked it up after the pub. It always goes down a treat with guests – I just have to remember which ones I have given it to already!

Serves 4

› 1 large grabbing handful of raisins or sultanas
› grated zest and juice of 1 large unwaxed orange
› 100ml whisky or Stone's ginger wine
› 1 McVitie's Jamaican Ginger Cake
› 40g unsalted butter
› 2 tablespoons honey
› clotted cream, to serve

1. Put the raisins or sultanas into a small saucepan with the orange zest and juice. Place over a medium heat and bring to a simmer, cooking the raisins or sultanas to the point where nearly all the orange juice has evaporated or been absorbed and the fruit has swollen. Pour in the booze and leave to one side to cool.

2. Half an hour before you are ready to make the puddings, preheat the oven to 190°C/fan 170°C/gas 5.

3. Peel back the paper from the sides of the ginger cake but don't remove it. Place it on a baking sheet and use the point of a knife to puncture 10 holes in the top. Smear the butter all over the top of the cake, then drizzle over the honey.

4. Bake the cake for approximately 15–18 minutes. When it comes out of the oven it should just be beginning to burn on the top and within minutes of being removed will be all crispy and caramelized.

5. Serve with clotted cream, and the raisins or sultanas in a little bowl.

'This always goes down a treat with guests – I just have to remember which ones I have given it to already!'

Fabulous gingery baked apples

This pudding is, I think, unwisely dismissed as old-fashioned or impoverished and better left behind. I disagree – it is one of the best there is.

Remember that if you don't have all the ingredients, you can simply replace them or leave them out. Swap the walnuts for hazelnuts, the sugar for honey, flip the rum for whisky... yadder, yadder, yadder... just don't get in the car and drive to the shops for prunes when you have raisins at home. Who knows, you may well find a combination that's better than this one. By all means flood the apples with custard, but I would advise a great clod of clotted cream instead.

Serves 4

› 4 medium Bramley apples
› clotted cream or custard, to serve

For the filling

› 4 balls of stem ginger in syrup, finely chopped
› 1 tablespoon peeled and grated fresh ginger
› grated zest of 1 unwaxed lemon
› 8 pitted prunes, finely chopped
› 2 heaped tablespoons dark muscovado sugar
› 1 tablespoon dark runny honey
› 4 ginger biscuits, crushed
› 2 tablespoons walnuts, preferably toasted, as the taste delivers more pleasure in this case
› 1 teaspoon ground allspice or cinnamon
› a good scratch of nutmeg
› a really generous splash of Lamb's navy rum or the like
› 70g fridge-cold unsalted butter, grated, or shredded suet
› flaked sea salt

1. Preheat the oven to 190°C/fan 170°C/gas 5 and line a baking tray with greaseproof paper.

2. Combine all the ingredients for the filling in a bowl, add a pinch of salt, and mix thoroughly.

3. Core the apples, then widen the holes considerably with the corer or paring knife and make a wide, slanted cut around the top of the hole, resembling a funnel opening, so as to ensure generous filling.

4. Run the blade of the knife around the outside middle of the apples just through their skin – like the equator around the globe, so to speak.

5. Put the apples on the prepared baking tray and stuff them generously with the prepared filling. Cover the stuffing with a small square of tin foil to prevent it from burning, and put the apples into the oven for 15–20 minutes. Remove the foil for the last 6 minutes or so of the cooking time to get a little crusting.

6. Remove the apples from the oven and serve immediately, with clotted cream or custard.

Poached pears in chocolate sauce

I used to love tinned pears with instant rubbish chocolate custard at school. But that was then and this is a little more elegant.

Serves 6

> 2 bay leaves
> 4 black peppercorns
> 1 long strip of lemon zest, removed with a potato peeler
> 500ml Sancerre or other white wine
> 200ml water
> 200g caster sugar
> 1 vanilla pod, split lengthways and seeds removed
> 6 Conference pears, ripe enough to own that pleasant smell of nail polish remover
> juice of 1 lemon
> 6 shortbread biscuits, to serve

For the sauce
> 100g plain dark chocolate (with at least 70% cocoa solids), broken into pieces (I like Lindt)
> 150ml double cream
> 4 tablespoons boiling water

1. Drop the bay leaves, peppercorns and lemon rind into a large saucepan and pour over the white wine and water. Tip in the sugar, then add the vanilla seeds, followed by the pod. Put the pan on the heat and bring to a very gentle simmer.

2. Meanwhile, peel the pears, leaving the stem attached. Very neatly cut out the little black core end from the bottom, then cut a thin sliver off the base to make it level and help the pears stand up on the plate. Sprinkle them with lemon juice.

3. Put the pears carefully into the saucepan and put a lid on the pan. Cook gently for approximately 20 minutes, until the pears are totally tender, turning them halfway through the cooking time and skimming off any scum. When the pears are ready, if you lift one by the stem it should not come away, yet a small sharp knife should slide into the pear easily with little pushing. If your pears were not sufficiently ripe, you may need to keep cooking them in instalments of 5 minutes. When they are done, remove them to a plate and allow them to cool.

4. Turn up the heat and simmer the pear liquor briskly with the pan uncovered, again skimming off any scum, for about 5 minutes, or until you achieve a consistency that will lightly coat the pears. (You should end up with around 350ml of liquid.) The syrup should be roughly similar in consistency to cough mixture.

5. Lay the pears in a Tupperware box or large bowl and pour the finished syrup all over the top of them. Chill them in the fridge, rolling them every now and then so they get syrup on all sides.

6. To make the sauce, put the broken chocolate pieces and the cream into a nonstick saucepan over a very low heat, stirring constantly, until the chocolate has almost completely melted but there are a few chunks still remaining. Do not allow the mixture to overheat. Remove from the heat and stir until completely melted. Add the boiling water and stir until smooth.

7. When ready to serve, reheat the sauce, stirring constantly. Spoon a lovely puddle of chocolate sauce on to each plate and stand a pear on top. Serve with a cheery little shortbread.

Caramelized bananas with butterscotch rum sauce

Probably my favourite pudding.

Serves 4

> › 20g unsalted butter
> › 4 bananas, peeled and halved lengthways
> › a glug of dark rum
> › 25ml double cream
> › grated zest of 1/2 unwaxed lime

For the butterscotch rum sauce

> › 100g caster sugar
> › 3–4 tablespoons water
> › 100ml double cream
> › 30g fridge-cold unsalted butter, cut into cubes
> › a glug of dark rum
> › juice of 1 lime
> › a generous pinch of grated nutmeg

1. To make the butterscotch rum sauce, heat a saucepan and add the sugar and water. Leave to caramelize over a medium heat, swirling the pan until the mixture starts to turn a dark golden colour. Once the caramel is golden, remove the saucepan from the heat and whisk in the cream, being careful of the spitting caramel.

2. When the cream is mixed in, add the butter, cube by cube, whisking as you go until the sauce is emulsified and glossy. Stir in the rum, then add the lime juice. Add the nutmeg, stir again, then leave the sauce to one side while you prepare the bananas.

3. Melt the butter in a heavy-based frying pan. Add the bananas, cut-side down. Cook over a medium heat in the frothing butter until their bases have gone dark golden and slightly crisp at the edges.

4. Flambé the pan with the rum and allow the contents to cook for about 30 seconds, then turn the bananas over and pour in the butterscotch rum sauce.

5. Finish the bananas with a swirl of cream and turn off the heat. Transfer to a serving bowl or platter and sprinkle over the lime zest. Serve immediately whilst the butterscotch sauce is still warm.

Richard's prunes

There is a brilliant baker and good friend of mine called Richard Bertinet. We have cooked together, shot together, fished together and eaten an unhealthy amount of pork rillettes together. So I thought it all right to ask him if I could include this devilish confection of his in my book. If you feed people enough of these prunes they freely blurt out the very information they have been trying to protect... Delicious yet deadly; good for a hearts-and-minds campaign.

Serves as many people as there are prunes

› 500g good prunes, stoned
› 1 bottle of cheap, rough dark rum

1. Put the prunes into a sterilized glass jar that is big enough to hold them snugly.

2. Pour in the rum so it comes up over the top of the prunes.

3. Seal the jar and leave it closed for 2 weeks. As the thirsty prunes soak up the grog, top the jar up with more rum.

4. Offer the prunes around. They are very good when eaten with cornichons and charcuterie, or with small strong coffees.

5. When the prunes are eaten, use the liquor for the next batch and top up with fresh rum.

6. Hic!

'Delicious yet deadly; good for a hearts-and-minds campaign.'

Apple-peel twigs

In the winter of 2012 I was invited by the Swedish tourist board to a dinner held in a private London house, as I had expressed an interest in Scandinavian cooking and was researching for a series I was about to start filming. The dinner was delicious. We started with roe, eggs of the tiny bleak fish, dolloped in greedy spoons on to crispbreads with crème fraîche, black pepper, shallots, dill and lemon. Then came a fabulously rich lamb stew accompanied by the largest mound of simply fried cep and trompette mushrooms I had seen so far. After that a Swedish apple crumble was served, one very different from our own, all crunchy and caramelized... and it was delicious too.

Despite the excellence of the whole dinner, particularly the bleak roe, it was these apple twigs that really stole the show for me because of their ingenuity. I am a great fan of getting as much to eat from my ingredients as possible, and these blew me away because I have never been more inventive with apple skins than adding them to the compost or flopping them in front of my sister's pig. This is one for any ration book of the future.

Although, when I had them, these were served with coffee, I think they would make a striking addition to a platter of sliced pork belly, or would work as a garnish with wild duck.

These apple twigs openly welcome different flavourings – ginger or clove and brown sugar, or maybe lavender with ground dried orange peel, are both good too.

Makes 4 apples' worth, or a heaped plateful

› ½ tablespoon icing sugar, plus extra for dusting
› ½ teaspoon ground cinnamon, plus extra for dusting
› peelings from 4 apples, such as Braeburn

1. Preheat the oven to 120°C/ fan 100°C/gas ½.

2. Sift the icing sugar and cinnamon over the peelings and lay them on a baking tray lined with greaseproof paper, making sure that, rather than just lying flat, they are twisted, but not over-manipulated, into relatively interesting shapes. Take care not to break them into strips that are too short.

3. Pop the peelings into the oven and bake until totally dried out and crisp, about 3–4 hours. They should be very brittle, with no pliancy, meaning unwanted moisture, at all.

4. Allow the twigs to cool completely, then, just before serving, dust them once more with icing sugar and a tad more cinnamon.

5. The twigs should be stored in an airtight container with a bit of kitchen paper in the bottom.

Figs in syrup

The scent of a fig tree is, I think, my favourite smell – as well as fresh marjoram, that is. It conjures images of Greece: the distant tinkle of goat bells and blinding sunlit white walls in steep villages. The fig fruit itself is not just delicious but furtive, succulent and raunchy. I'm surprised it was not the fig that Eve was blamed for, for twisting it from its milky stalk. These jarred figs are delicious eaten for breakfast on Greek yoghurt, with a silty little coffee on the side. The fruits must be good ones, otherwise don't bother.

Makes 1 x 1.5-litre jar

› 100g soft brown sugar
› 100g caster sugar
› 200g dark runny honey
› 200ml water
› 1 teaspoon orange flower water (optional)
› 12 figs, 3 vertical slits made in the skin of each

1. Put the sugars, honey and water into a large saucepan and bring it up to a simmer until the sugar has dissolved. Add the orange flower water (if using).

2. Drop the figs into the saucepan and bring them up to a gentle simmer for 20 minutes.

3. Transfer the figs to a large sterilized Kilner jar, cover with the syrup and screw on the lid. It is important that the syrup completely covers the figs.

4. Allow to cool. The figs will keep for 1 month or so, but use them within 3 or 4 days once opened.

'The fig fruit is not just delicious but furtive, succulent and raunchy.'

Notes on fruit salad

This is not a recipe but rather a guideline. I can be a real bore on the subject and here goes. Generally, every time a glass bowl of fruit salad is plonked on the table my heart sinks, as I expect it to be followed by a jug of evaporated milk (which, come to think of it, does have a place in a mango milkshake – please see my previous book, *The Good Table*). Note to my mother-in-law: you are an exception to the rule – I love your fruit salad.

I'll keep it brief. A fruit salad containing apples, oranges, grapefruit, furry watermelon, slimy bananas and crumbling kiwi fruit makes me lose the will to live. Not all the above-mentioned fruit (i.e. banana and kiwi) are a bad idea but they must be added only just before serving. Apple segments with the skin left on and pithy orange segments just remind me of school. If you are adding oranges, the fruit segments must be released of all pith and inner skin. Mandarins take precedence over oranges, but peeling off their little segment skins is a real labour of love/bore. Passion fruits wake up a salad no end, as do really acidic, sweet pears with that peardrop taste. Pineapple must be fresh, not tinned, and ripe like the mangoes. If you can find Alphonso mangoes with their techno-orange flesh, you have made the salad even better. I love papaya, but good fragrant ones are hard to find and many people detest this fruit anyway. Grenadine, used as the sweetener, is a good replacement for straight sugar. I like adding pomegranate seeds too, but you may find things a bit seedy, what with the passion fruit. I, however, like this. Lime juice and zest catapult a fruit salad into something mouth-watering.

Finish with a grating of nutmeg over the top. Resist the urge to steep everything in a carton of fruit juice as, without it, in not much time the salad will be swimming in its own lovely blood. The more in advance a fruit salad is made, the less it will deliver; the only time it needs to rest before eating is the time it takes for it to become cold in the fridge.

Fruit salad encourages the fantasy that you are on holiday, a distraction in our cruel winter months. The thick coconut cream that often separates from the water in a tin is good mixed with double cream to serve alongside the salad. I like my salad with nothing on top. The remaining milky coconut water can be used in the curry you serve before this pudding. I leave the rest to you.

Any juice left in the salad is good strained and mixed with dark rum, Angostura bitters, ginger ale and lime juice, with ice and a scratch of nutmeg, for a killer Planter's Punch.

Wisty's apple cake

I asked my wife for this recipe. She replied, 'I'll give it to you once you've finished your book, as there is no urgency for me to write one recipe when you still have a hundred to do.' I was intending to call it Charlotte's Apple Cake, as it is was always she who baked it, but when I finally opened Charlotte's email it said the recipe had in fact been sent by her mother, or Wisty, as we all call her.

I love the fact that this illustrates the handing-on of recipes in a family, a practice so important for any culture but fast disappearing from our own. Here is my mother-in-law's recipe directly from the email, written in good old imperial measurements.

Serves 6-8

› 2 large free-range eggs
› 9oz caster sugar, plus extra for sprinkling
› 3³/4oz unsalted butter
› just over 1/4 pint top of the milk (or 2/3 milk and 1/3 cream)
› 6¹/2oz plain flour
› 2 rounded teaspoons baking powder
› 3 or 4 smallish Bramley cooking apples, peeled, cored and sliced
› icing sugar, for dusting

1. Preheat the oven to 375°F and line a 12 × 16-inch roasting tin or cake tin with baking parchment.

2. Whisk the eggs with the sugar until the whisk leaves a trail when it is lifted out of the mixture.

3. Put the butter and milk (or milk and cream) into a pan and bring to the boil, then stir the liquid into the eggs and sugar.

4. Fold in the flour and baking powder, mixing thoroughly. Pour the mixture into the baking tin.

5. Arrange the apples over the mixture. Sprinkle with caster sugar.

6. Bake the cake in the oven for 20–25 minutes.

7. Allow to cool, then dust with a little icing sugar.

'I love the fact that this illustrates the handing-on of recipes in a family.'

Index

Acknowledgements

Thank you to everyone who supports me as, after all, it's you who help me continue to do this job that I love.

Chris Terry – Always a pleasure! Whether swilling Campari, eating quivering wibbly bits of unknown bollito misto or putting down plates of food before your camera. You're a talent, you're a pro, you're a friend, you could be a comedian.

Dan – Hawk man. There you perch on the post like a kestrel. You watch, you twitch, you swoop, and it's 'done already'. Chris is a lucky photographer to have such an assistant. The '2 stone tooth' still makes me burst out laughing at inappropriate times.

Denise Bates – Thank you for being not simply my publisher but also someone who clearly supports their writers in both their work and personal life. Nevertheless it's probably good that whenever I approach your office I feel like I used to when summoned by the headmaster.

Pene Parker – You're fab! It's that simple, and thank you too for your understanding and camaraderie.

Tracey Smith – Having you in the room means a day of laughter is guaranteed. Always positive, always smiling. Please clone yourself at the earliest opportunity.

Leanne Bryan – For your gentleness, carefulness and keen eyes, both of which I have returned.

The Mitchell Beazley production team – Thank you for your all your care and hard work.

Katie Giovanni and team – Thank you for being really organized and making it simple, even when I changed my mind... a lot.

Justine Pattison and Lauren Brignell (Batman and Robin) – Love your work and trust you both! In fact, enough to relax when I know you're involved. Thank you, Jus, for teaching me a better spoon-to-pen system. Lauren, you are an asset to any situation. Your lashings of common sense are invaluable. Thank you for your contribution to this book.

Becki Wallington, my PA – Thanks for sorting out the washing basket of tangled recipes and missing bits like separated socks, and for keeping everyone in sync.

Annie Lee – Thank you, sharp eyes!

Charlotte – Thank you for your cool head and sense.

Minnie and Louis – Thanks to my little ones, whom I strive for and learn from.

Mother Nature – Can happily live with you, can't live without you.